The Social Psychology of Behaviour in Small Groups

'a very welcome addition to the literature on small groups. The style is lively, and there are frequent suggestions for short mental exercises that encourage active learning, keep the reader alert and encourage relating the text to one's own experience.'

Herb Blumberg, Goldsmiths College, University of London

'. . . an extremely well balanced and readable book. . . . I shall certainly be recommending it to my students.'

Phil Erwin, Edge Hill College, Lancashire

The Social Psychology of Behaviour in Small Groups covers theories of group behaviour and their application in organisational psychology. Topics include the structure and formation of groups and the roles that individuals play within groups, as well as more applied areas such as co-operation and conflict, teamwork, leadership and decision-making in small groups. Donald Pennington has provided a lively, accessible and systematic text suitable for undergraduates studying social psychology and those studying organisational psychology on psychology and business studies courses.

Professor Donald Pennington is Pro-Vice-Chancellor of Coventry University. His areas of interest include social psychology, health psychology and personality. He is an Associate Fellow of the British Psychological Society and the author of several textbooks in social psychology.

Psychology Focus

Series editor: Perry Hinton, University of Luton

The Psychology Focus series provides students with a new focus on key topic areas in psychology. It supports students taking modules in psychology, whether for a psychology degree or a combined programme, and those renewing their qualification in a related discipline. Each short book:

- presents clear, in-depth coverage of a discrete area with many applied examples
- assumes no prior knowledge of psychology
- has been written by an experienced teacher
- has chapter summaries, annotated further reading and a glossary of key terms.

Also available in this series:

The Social Psychology of Behaviour in Small Groups

■ Donald C Pennington

First published 2002
by Psychology Press Ltd
27 Church Road, Hove, East Sussex
BN3 2FA
www.psypress.co.uk

Simultaneously published in
the USA and Canada
by Taylor & Francis, Inc.
29 West 35th Street,
New York, NY 10001

Psychology Press is part of the Taylor & Francis Group

© 2002 Donald C. Pennington

Typeset in Sabon and Futura by
Florence Production Ltd, Stoodleigh,
Devon

Printed and bound in Great Britain by
TJ International Ltd, Padstow,
Cornwall
Cover design by Terry Foley

British Library Cataloguing in Publication Data
A catalogue record for this book is
available from the British Library

Library of Congress Cataloging-in-Publication Data

Pennington, Donald C.
   The social psychology of behaviour
in small groups/Donald C.
Pennington.
      p. cm – (Psychology Focus)
   Includes bibliographical references
and index.
   ISBN 0–415–23098–5 –
ISBN 0–415–23099–3 (pbk)
      1. Small groups—Psychological
aspects. 2. Social Psychology.
   3. Organisational behaviour.
      I. Title II. Series

HM736.P46 2002
302.3'4—dc21

ISBN 0–415–23098–5 (hbk)
ISBN 0–415–23099–3 (pbk)

Contents

Illustrations

Figures

Tables

Series preface

The Psychology Focus series provides short, up-to-date accounts of key areas in psychology without assuming the reader's prior knowledge in the subject. Psychology is often a favoured subject area for study, since it is relevant to a wide range of disciplines such as Sociology, Education, Nursing and Business Studies. These relatively inexpensive but focused short texts combine sufficient detail for psychology specialists with sufficient clarity for non-specialists.

The series authors are academics experienced in undergraduate teaching as well as research. Each takes a topic within their area of psychological expertise and presents a short review, highlighting important themes and including both theory and research findings. Each aspect of the topic is clearly explained with supporting glossaries to elucidate technical terms.

The series has been conceived within the context of the increasing modularisation which has been developed in higher education over the last decade and fulfils the consequent need for clear, focused, topic-based course material. Instead of following one course of study, students on a modularisation programme are often able to choose modules from a wide range of disciplines to complement the modules they are required to study for a specific degree. It can no longer be assumed that students studying a particular module will necessarily have the same background knowledge (or lack of it!) in that subject. But they will need to familiarise themselves with a particular topic rapidly since a single module in a single topic may be only 15 weeks long, with assessments arising during that period. They may have to combine eight or more modules in a single year to obtain a degree at the end of their programme of study.

One possible problem with studying a range of separate modules is that the relevance of a particular topic or the relationship between topics may not always be apparent. In the Psychology Focus series, authors have drawn where possible on practical and applied examples to support the points being made so that readers can see the wider relevance of the topic under study. Also, the study of psychology is usually broken up into separate areas, such as social psychology, developmental psychology and cognitive psychology, to take three examples. Whilst the books in the Psychology Focus series will provide excellent coverage of certain key topics within these 'traditional' areas, the authors have not been constrained in their examples and explanations and may draw on material across the whole field of psychology to help explain the topic under study more fully.

Each text in the series provides the reader with a range of important material on a specific topic. They are suitably comprehensive and give a clear account of the important issues involved. The authors analyse and interpret the material as well as present an up-to-date and detailed review of key work. Recent references are provided along with suggested further reading to allow readers to investigate the topic in more depth. It is hoped, therefore, that after following the informative review of a key topic in a Psychology Focus text, readers not only will have a clear understanding of the issues in question but will be intrigued and challenged to investigate the topic further.

Acknowledgements

I have wanted to write a text on the social psychology of behaviour in small groups for a number of years. Some of the topics covered in this book are sadly neglected in general social psychology textbooks, so I hope this book fills a gap.

I have also enjoyed writing this book, the more so since most of it was written at a table in a bay window of a house overlooking the harbour in Porthleven, Cornwall. At times my daughter, Kyla, and sons, Tom and Jed, were with me and dragged me down to the pubs in the evenings. So thanks to Kyla, Tom and Jed.

I would like to thank Perry Hinton, the series editor, for advice, support and helpful comments on the first draft of this book. So thanks to Perry. I would also like to thank two anonymous reviewers who provided helpful and detailed comments on the first draft of this text. The comments of Perry and the anonymous reviewers have helped to improve the book enormously.

ACKNOWLEDGEMENTS

My thanks also to Kathleen Williams who typed, formatted and advised on styles and layouts for the book, particularly the figures. So thanks to Kathleen for doing such a great job.

The author and publisher wish to thank The Free Press for permission to reproduce the SYMLOG Adjective Rating Scale from SYMLOG: A System for the Multiple Level Observation of Groups by Robert F. Bales, Stephen P. Cohen, with the assistance of Stephen A. Williamson. Copyright © 1979 The Free Press.

To Blob, of course, and Isobel

Chapter 1

Introduction to the social psychology of behaviour in small groups

Introduction

I MAGINE THE WORLD one hundred years into the future; the use of electronic communications technology has developed to a point where people no longer meet and interact in face-to-face situations. Groups of people do not come together as a project team, work group, leisure group or self-help group. All communication and interaction is done electronically through computers. Would you enjoy living in such a world? Psychologically, do you think you would miss interaction with other people and working with others and interacting face-to-face in a small group?

Who knows where the world of electronics will take us and what the psychological consequences will be. However, if you think about it, this extreme picture of a possible future world starkly shows just how much of our life at work, at home and in leisure activities centres around being a part of a small group of people. This book provides an introduction to the social psychology of small group behaviour, based on a world in which face-to-face interaction in small groups is a central and important feature of most aspects of each of our lives.

In this chapter we will look at some of the fundamentals of small groups: definitions of and different types of small groups; why people join groups and different types of group membership; communication in small groups; and the physical, social and temporal environment of small groups. These topics are dealt with in this first chapter since they underly the particular topics related to behaviour in small groups that are dealt with in subsequent chapters.

What are small groups?

To understand better what social psychologists consider to represent small groups we will take a number of different perspectives. First, a definition will be suggested to provide guidance as to what may be regarded as a small group for social psychological purposes; second, we will see how groups may be classified along a formal–informal dimension; third, two different types of groups, self-help groups and work groups, will be looked at more closely.

Definitions

This book is about the social psychology of small group behaviour, and since the term 'group' may be widely applied to describe a wide range of different collections of people, some definitional considerations will prove useful. One distinction that can readily be made is between aggregates of people and a *psychological group* (Buchanan and Huczynski, 1997). These are defined as follows:

- A *psychological group* is any number of people who interact with each other, are psychologically aware of each other and perceive themselves to be in a group.
- An *aggregate* is a collection of unrelated people who happen to be in close proximity for a short period of time.

First, the important features of a psychological group concern interaction between members of the group. This interaction may be face-to-face, through tele-conferencing with a video link and through other electronic means such as e-mail. The point is that meaningful interactions, perhaps not necessarily verbal, take place between group members. Second, each member of the group is aware of other group members and the number of other people in the group. Finally, each of the group members must know that they are members of a particular group. Given this definition, consider the following list and identify which you think represents a psychological group based on this definition:

1   the audience watching a film at the cinema
2   members of a hockey team
3   a jury retiring to agree a verdict in a criminal case
4   people in the same carriage on a train journey
5   a Government committee, such as the Cabinet
6   a project team in a large organisation.

How did you do? The definitions given above would mean that (1) and (4) would be an aggregate of people and (2), (3), (5) and (6) a psychological group. Notice, however, that with (4) there may be some travellers in the train carriage who form a psychological group.

This definition of a psychological group would allow very large groups – for instance, all people working for a large organisation such as Coventry University – to be classified as a psychological group. This book is about *small groups*, which has been taken to mean between two and up to 30 members. It is difficult to be precise about the upper limit, but beyond 30 (perhaps over 20) a group becomes difficult to manage and to prevent from breaking into smaller subgroups. In this book the most common size of group, and examples used, varies between three or four to 15 or 20 group members.

Additional defining features of psychological groups that are of interest to social psychologists include the group having shared goals and a structure. Shared goals of the group should normally be agreed upon by group members. It is also usually assumed that the goals are best achieved or may only be achieved by a small group rather than an individual working alone. Reference to group structure includes such things as norms and rules, a leader or leaders, followers and roles of individual group members (see Chapter 3).

Formal and informal groups

Jennifer works for a local authority council as part of a group dealing with planning applications for new houses, extensions and so on. In addition, Jennifer is a member of a group of employees of the council who all have an interest in keeping fit, and regularly go as a group to the local fitness centre. The first group described here is a *formal group* and the second an *informal group*; these may be defined as follows:

- *Formal groups* are created by an organisation to help achieve its collective purpose or mission. Formal groups are set organisational tasks and are held responsible for their achievements.
- *Informal groups* are collections of individuals who have a common interest and develop interdependencies, influence each other's behaviours and contribute to mutual need satisfaction (Buchanan and Huczynski, 1997).

Formal groups tend to be task-oriented, endure over time, have a formal structure and are recognised as a defined group by the organisation and other formal groups in the organisation.

Informal groups develop and exist to meet more personal needs of individuals such as belongingness, good social relationships, sharing common interests and so on. Usually an organisation does not plan such groups, but would encourage their development, as long as they did not interfere with work, to foster greater employee satisfaction and motivation.

To highlight the distinction and points made here you might find it useful to think about an organisation you know about and, if appropriate, work in. Try to identify the formal and informal groups – you should find that most informal groups have to do with leisure activities and common interests of staff in the organisation.

Work groups

Formal work groups are normally task-oriented and usually clear about the task that has been set the group. The words 'normally' and 'usually' are deliberately used here since a formal group may allow relationships in the group to take priority over the task (for example, see Chapter 7 – Groupthink) or not be certain what its task or purpose is (for example, see Chapter 6 – Leadership). With these caveats in mind work groups have to deal with a number of issues as depicted in Table 1.1 (Chapters 3 to 7 consider these in more detail). You may wonder how small groups can be effective given that so many different issues have to be considered and dealt with.

An approach different from that common in western organisations is the Japanese approach to work groups. Rather than have a primary focus on roles, functions and group structure, the Japanese analyse group processes in terms of cohesion, consensus and morality (Pascale and Athos, 1982). Of particular importance in a Japanese work group is the acceptance of the leader by all group members. While task matters are important, the leader is highly sensitive to maintaining the well-being of the group as a whole and the relationships between individual group members. Quite often in western work groups task achievement and performance override all other considerations. The Japanese approach clearly recognises that for a group to achieve its tasks and objectives it must be functional rather than dysfunctional at an interpersonal level. Recognising this, the Japanese tend to encourage small work groups of between eight and 12 people. Groups of this size ensure that all members are able to relate and communicate with other group members and to be aware of what is happening at an interpersonal level.

Self-help groups

Self-help groups present a clear contrast with work groups since they are voluntary groupings of people who come together with the main purpose of allowing needs and problems to be shared. Self-help groups became very popular throughout the 1990s and an extremely wide range of such groups exist, representing, for example, health groups, classic car groups, people who have suffered as victims of crime and so on. The list is virtually endless

TABLE 1.1 Issues and questions facing any work group

Issue	Questions to be answered
Atmosphere and relations	Should the group be formal or informal? How friendly or work-like should relationships be?
Member participation	Should all group members participate equally or some more than others?
Goal understanding and acceptance	Do all group members clearly need to understand the goals of the group? Should all group members be committed to the goals of the group?
Listening and information sharing	How is information to be shared? Do all group members need to know everything?
Disagreements and conflicts	How should conflict and disagreements be handled? Do all conflicts need to be resolved?
Decision-making	How should decisions be made – through consensus, majority decision or by the leader?
Evaluation of performance	How should group and member evaluation be carried out? Should the leader or all group members take responsibility?
Expression of feelings	Should members be allowed to express feelings openly and directly?
Division of labour	How are individual tasks to be assigned to group members?
Leadership	Who should lead the group? How should the leader be appointed? What are the functions of the leader?

Source: adapted from Cohen *et al.* (1995)

and, with the development of the internet, self-help groups have moved from being more locally based and characterised by face-to-face interaction, to being national and global with electronic communication. Perhaps the self-help group that many people cite as an example is AA (Alcoholics Anonymous), which has a long-established history.

Over 20 years ago, Levy (1979) provided a four-fold classification of self-help groups that is still applicable today. The four categories are:

1   behavioural-control or conduct-reorganisation groups
2   stress-coping and support groups
3   survival-oriented groups
4   personal growth and self-actualisation groups.

Typical examples of behavioural-control groups are Alcoholics Anonymous and Weight Watchers. The purpose of such groups is to control a behaviour problem common to all members. Stress-coping and support groups include many health-oriented groups. Survival-oriented groups include groups of people discriminated against by society due to, for example, sexual orientation, race or social class. Finally, personal growth groups represent groupings of people who want to improve or enhance themselves in some way. See if you can correctly categorise the following self-help groups.

- gamblers anonymous
- gay activist group
- achieving your potentials group
- parents without partners
- breast cancer self-help group
- Christian faith group.

(NB: these are largely imaginary groups created to help you understand the classifications better.)

Self-help groups develop group norms, have rules (usually) about how they operate, often require formal membership with criteria for membership, set goals, and have interaction among group members. These topics are explored more fully in the following chapters of this book. Self-help groups are rightly regarded as psychological groups (see the definition given in section 1.2.1 above) and, while many are very large with national or international profiles, they usually operate at local levels in small face-to-face meetings (Wuthnow, 1994).

Joining groups and group membership

We are all members of groups, whether those groups are formal or informal. Not all the groups we are members of would count as psychological groups – for example, the group of people who have blue eyes. Sometimes we have a choice about whether or not to join a group and in other ways we have little or no choice. Here we explore a little more why people join groups and the types of group membership that can be identified.

Why do people join groups?

People usually have more choice and can decide for themselves about joining informal groups compared to formal and more work-related groups. In work settings people appointed to work for an organisation are usually assigned to an established group. However, when taskforces or working groups are set up for a specified period of time and given a particular task or brief, there is often opportunity to volunteer or be selected for such groups. Opportunity to join such a group might have to do with particular expertise that the individual has to offer (task or interpersonal) or because some criteria of representativeness across the organisation are being followed. People may apply to join a work group and not be successful, or may be selected by someone more senior in the organisation.

The picture with informal groups is different. People largely choose to join leisure groups, self-help groups, common interest groups and so on. However, with a self-help group such as Alcoholics Anonymous or Gamblers Anonymous it may be that others are making the choice for you, or you are being persuaded or coerced to join! The main reasons why people join informal groups are: security; to enhance self-esteem; to share information and/or gain knowledge; affiliation and fulfilment of social needs; and to achieve certain goals or objectives (Napier and Gershenfeld, 1999).

Informal groups can offer the member security, since people feel more able to stand up to others in a difficult situation in the company of others or better able to share the same problem or concerns. In addition, other people, groups or organisations are more likely to listen to a group than to an individual. Joining an informal group can enhance a person's self-esteem since, for example, knowledge may be gained or self-doubts that an individual thinks specific to him or her may be found to be common to all people in the group. This provides reassurance that a person is not alone, so it also relates to the security function. Fulfilment of social needs reflects the fact that people are social creatures and need to be with other people. Enjoyment comes from social interaction with others and the development of successful, meaningful relationships in life relates to good mental health. Finally, groups help share the work and achieve challenging or difficult objectives more easily than working alone.

Types of membership

Membership of both formal and informal groups, work groups and self-help groups may itself be formal or informal. This might sound confusing, so for the purposes of the following discussion we will use the terms 'official' and 'unofficial' with regard to membership of formal or informal groups. Table 1.2 provides the four types of membership with examples generated by these distinctions.

Other types of membership, apart from official and unofficial, also exist. For example, a person may be an aspiring member of a group – this may be common where someone wants to join an exclusive golf or tennis club and has to enter their name on a waiting list. Another type of membership is a marginal member of a group. Here, for example, a working group or taskforce may have been established to introduce computer networking into an organisation. Someone with very specialist expert skills may only be called upon by the group on occasions when that type of expert input is required. Another way to look at marginal membership is to use the distinction between active involvement in the group or membership that is passive. An example of this might be membership of a local branch of the Labour Party. You could

TABLE 1.2 Types of membership and groups with examples of each

	Official membership	Unofficial membership
Formal group	**Formal-official** Committee in an organisation with distinct categories of the membership required	**Formal-unofficial** Working group or task-force in an organisation. Membership may change over time
Informal group	**Informal-official** Self-help group such as Weight Watchers requires subscription	**Informal-unofficial** Self-help group, such as specific type of health group, not requiring subscription or regular attendance

be an active member participating in meetings, campaigns and door-to-door hustings at elections, or a passive member paying the annual subscription but never or only rarely attending meetings of the local branch.

As an exercise, list three groups of which you are a member and determine which of the following categories you think you fall into:

- official member or unofficial member
- central member or marginal member
- informal group or formal group
- free to choose to join or not free to choose to join
- have expert input or do not have expert input.

In conducting this exercise you also become aware that you are a member of many groups, certainly more than three! At times, however, multiple membership can bring conflicts as well. For example, suppose you work for a tobacco company and are also against smoking and a member of ASH (the anti-smoking pressure group). Could you live with such a conflict or would you have to remove yourself from working in either the tobacco company or ASH? Generally, people do try to avoid conflicts resulting from membership of different groups, but this is not always possible.

Communication in small groups

The definition of a small psychological group, given earlier, highlighted social interaction as a key feature. Fundamental to social interaction is communication between members of a small group as well as communication with others outside of the group. In what follows we shall mostly concentrate on intragroup communication, i.e. within the group.

The communication process

Communication may be defined as the process by which an individual (or group of individuals) transmits information about ideas, feelings and intentions to another person (or group of people). Communication in groups may serve functions which include controlling group members, expressing emotions, motivating others and exchanging information. This characterisation highlights three key aspects of communication. First an individual's wishes to communicate with another – the former is usually called the sender and the latter the receiver. Second, the communication may be transmitted through a range of different media, such as verbal, non-verbal, written, electronic. Third, while one or more media may be used to transmit the communication, there may be 'noise' used in the media system that distorts or makes the message difficult to interpret on the part of the receiver. Thus the message or communication that the sender intended to make may not be the message that is received. The receivers also have perceptions and may interpret the communication to suit themselves or consistent with their own expectations. This introduces another source of distortion to the communication the sender intended to make. Finally, in addition to these features of communication, a feedback loop needs to be added. This allows the receiver of the message to indicate it has been received, but also how it has been interpreted. The

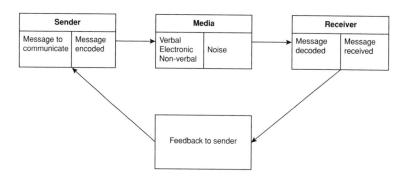

FIGURE 1.1 The encoder–decoder model of communication

receiver then communicates back to the sender and so on – reflecting continual communication and social interaction in a group. Figure 1.1 depicts the main aspects of what has been said above.

Barriers to communication

If communication were as simple as shown in Figure 1.1 then it would take place smoothly, with the message the sender intended to make correctly interpreted by the receiver. Unfortunately this is often not the case and communications are found to be easily misunderstood or misinterpreted. There are many explanations and reasons for this. Here we will focus on just four: selective perception, emotions, language, and non-verbal cues. In section 1.4.3 we look more at the effect of different communication structures on communication.

Imagine you are trying to describe the good experience you had when on holiday in Cornwall – how nice the weather was, how you had found the service good in restaurants and how friendly everybody was to you. Now consider being the other person who had been on holiday in Cornwall last year when it rained for the week, restaurants were crowded and service slow. You would no doubt interpret the very positive account in light of your bad experience. This example serves to highlight the fact that (1) people bring past experiences and pre-existing knowledge to bear on interpreting a message, and (2) parts of the message may be selectively attended to. For example, suppose in the positive account of the holiday you also said that traffic was bad and parking difficult. The person who experienced the bad holiday may give this more weight in their interpretation of what you are saying since it fits in better with their own experience. In general, people often interpret messages to fit in or add confirmation to their own, sometime idiosyncratic, experiences.

Emotions can clearly colour how you interpret a communication. If you are in a happy mood you are more likely to see the positive side of things. If you are in an angry or depressed mood you are more likely to interpret the communication in a negative way. People rarely come to a communication as emotionally neutral, and one of the skills of a good communicator will be accurately to judge the emotional state a person is in and tailor the message accordingly.

How you use language affects how people interpret a communication. For example, if you speak in a formal way using technical terms and in the 'Queen's English', you may be perceived as being highly official, somewhat unapproachable and cold, and very task-oriented. If, by contrast, you speak casually, using slang or more informal phrases such as 'cool', you may be perceived as approachable, warm, but perhaps more concerned with relationships than with the task. Something of this is captured by Bales' *Interaction Process Analysis* (1950), which is a method of measuring group behaviour (see Chapter 2 of this book).

In face-to-face interaction there is a rich and diverse range of non-verbal cues that are used to interpret the communication. These include eye contact, body orientation, dress, smiles or frowns, interpersonal distance and so on. There are also cues such as rate of speaking, being softly or loudly spoken, hesitant or fluent, and emotionally tinged with sadness, happiness and so on. How you convey your message non-verbally can affect, for example, how confident you are perceived to be about what you are saying, how sincere you are, and even whether you are seen to be telling the truth or lying (see Pennington *et al.*, 1999, for a more detailed consideration of non-verbal communication).

Facilitating communication

Using the model shown in Figure 1.1, four entities present them-selves to help facilitate communication: the sender, the media, the receiver, and the feedback given. Space precludes treatment of all of these – here we will focus on the sender and receiver.

If you have ever had the experience of filling in a tax form you may think that the instructions were incomprehensible. You may well be right! Although it sounds easy, the golden rules for the sender are to keep the message simple and free of jargon. The common use of acronyms (for example, NIMBY – Not In My Back Yard) are often specific to a particular context – education, busi-ness, subcultures and so on. People who use the same acronyms every day become unaware of this, and when communicating with 'outsiders' they often wonder why there is a look of puzzlement and lack of understanding on the other person's face.

From the point of view of the receiver, he or she should try to avoid interpreting the message in just one way and look for wider meanings. In addition, the receiver needs to demonstrate that he or she is a good listener and hence provide feedback to the sender. Good listening skills are very important to the sender since this will permit an assessment of whether or not the message is being interpreted in the way intended. The point being made here is that effective small group communication is highly dependent on people having good communication skills.

Communication networks

Up to this point our consideration of communication has assumed that people have been free to communicate with each other in a small group in a largely uncontrolled and unstructured way. However, small groups may have a *communication structure* imposed on them, thereby restricting who can communicate with whom in a group. Bavelas (1950) investigated the effects of impos-ing certain communication restrictions, called *communication networks*, on the speed and accuracy with which groups solved problems, and measured members' satisfaction with the restrictions

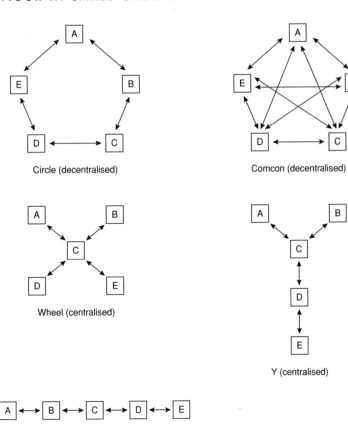

FIGURE 1.2 Examples of five-person communication networks. Boxes represent individual positions and arrows permissible communications between individuals in the network

Source: after Bavelas (1950)

of a specific communication network. The five most commonly researched communication networks are given in Figure 1.2.

These networks vary in the extent to which communication between group members is centralised or decentralised. The Y, wheel and the chain represent the most centralised networks, since communications from individuals at the extreme positions all have to go through a central person. The decentralised networks are the circle and comcon. In these networks individuals have a greater number of people with whom each can communicate and there is no one central position in the network.

Bavelas and Barrett (1951), and Leavitt (1951) experimentally investigated these different networks through giving groups problem-solving tasks. Measures of time taken to solve a problem and accuracy at solving the problem were recorded. Individuals in a network were asked how satisfied they were with working in the group and whether a leader had emerged. The findings are summarised in Table 1.3. As can be seen, the decentralised networks of the chain and comcon received high satisfaction ratings from individual members with no leader emerging. However, speed of solving the problem was slow in the circle and fast in the comcon. In the circle there is restricted communication, in the comcon everyone is free to communicate with the rest of the group. For the decentralised networks – chain, wheel and Y – speed and accuracy at problem-solving were good, and in each a leader was perceived to emerge. However, individual satisfaction was only moderate to low.

In terms of the type of task or problems set to these five communication networks, centralised networks were found to be faster and more accurate on simple tasks, while decentralised networks were faster and more accurate on complex tasks. The most likely explanation of this has to do with saturation. Centralised networks on complex tasks demand too much of the central person, and he or she quickly becomes saturated with information and requests. By contrast, in decentralised networks information can be

TABLE 1.3 Task performance, leader emergence and individual satisfaction resulting from the five communication networks

Measure taken	Chain	Y	Wheel	Circle	Concom
Speed	Moderate	Moderate	Fast	Slow	Fast
Accuracy	High	High	High	Low	Moderate
Leader emerges	Moderate	Moderate	High	None	None
Satisfaction	Moderate	Moderate	Low	High	High

Source: adapted from Leavitt (1951)

distributed and co-ordinated by each member of the group, thus avoiding one person becoming overloaded or saturated.

Research on communication networks demonstrates the effect of imposing certain communication lines between members of a small group. These can affect both performance and individual satisfaction of working in the group.

Electronic communication

Electronic communication is not new – Morse code has been around for over a hundred years. However, with computer technology providing e-mail, the internet, video-conferencing, voice mail and so on, access and use has been taken up by all organisations and by many people at home. For example, by the middle of 2000, about 60 per cent of homes in Finland, 40 per cent in the United States of America and 30 per cent in Great Britain had e-mail and access to the internet. Growth rates in the first decade of the twenty-first century are expected to be dramatic. While systems such as e-mail enable fast communication between people and allow groups to work with individuals who are geographically separate, it is important to ask whether or not electronic communication is effective. Kiesler and Sproull (1992) found that groups communicating electronically took longer to reach a unanimous decision compared to groups who communicated through face-to-face interaction. Dubrovsky *et al.* (1991) found that e-mail served to reduce status differentials between individuals in a group. Video-conferencing does allow all individuals in the group to see each other and communicate from a distance.

The use of electronic communication is set to grow dramatically over the next few years. As more and more people become comfortable with using such means of communication, we should expect greater efficiency and effectiveness by small groups.

The environment of small groups

The main focus of this book has to do with what takes place within small groups and how groups perform. However, it is important to remember that groups do not operate in a vacuum, detached from their social and environmental context. One important context is the culture in which the group is embedded. This will be considered in section 1.6. Here we will look at three aspects of the environment of small groups that have been regarded as important and extensively researched (Levine and Moreland, 1995). These are physical, social and temporal factors.

The physical environment

Physical factors such as lighting levels, temperature, amount of space or degree of crowding, and noise levels have all been identified as factors which can affect group performance, satisfaction of group members and group interaction (Sundstrom, 1986). For example, when a group is crowded together and operating in high temperatures, individual members of the group tend to act negatively and with a degree of hostility towards each other (Griffit, 1970).

In extreme environments, such as working underwater or as astronauts in space, groups tend to be characterised by strong leadership, high cohesiveness and high levels of conformity (Kanas, 1985). These characteristics are functional in such extreme environments since they facilitate co-ordinated behaviour in the group, a reduction in conflict between group members and high levels of trust among each other. In extreme environments newcomers to a group often have to go through quite severe initiation ceremonies. Such rituals serve to impress upon the newcomer that his or her safety is dependent on others in the group, and for the established group members to assess the newcomer (Vaught and Smith, 1980).

Another aspect of the physical environment is the seating arrangement of the group. Key (1986), for example, showed that communication and productivity are likely to be enhanced if members of the group sit in a circle.

The social environment

Small groups do not operate in social isolation; there are often other groups who offer competition or co-operation, and influences from significant or powerful individuals. The social psychology of intergroup relations is not dealt with in this book – excellent treatments exist elsewhere (e.g. Brown, 2000). Small groups also exist within organisational structures of some sort – whether formal as in work groups or informal as in family groups. Organisations should provide an environment that supports and facilitates the work of a small group. However, a feature identified of unsuccessful organisations is that they may weaken and present barriers to groups working effectively (Krantz, 1985). Groups in both formal and informal structures are able to exercise some control by bargaining with others for resources, obtaining information, defending themselves against outside influences and creating a positive impression with others (Ancona and Caldwell, 1988).

Small groups may also contain individuals who are not group members but who can have a significant influence over the group. Such individuals include prospective and ex-members, customers, clients and enemies. The presence of hostile others or enemies of the group causes the group to become more cohesive, forget about differences for a while and close ranks. This is especially the case if a hostile person threatens the very existence of the group (Reitzes and Diver, 1982).

The temporal environment

Groups vary greatly in the length of time they stay together. Some groups come together only once or occasionally (for example, a jury); other groups meet over a period of time and on a number of different occasions (for example, taskforces or project teams). In contrast, other groups exist over a period of years or even decades (for example, the Cabinet). Groups that only meet on one or two occasions usually maintain the same membership. However, as the longevity of a group increases, changes in membership and leadership are common and to be expected. Indeed, a change of government as a result of a general election will transform the membership of the Cabinet.

Groups that exist over a period of time show distinct patterns of development, and new members who join established groups are socialised into the norms and rules of the group. These matters are dealt with more fully in Chapter 4.

When long-established groups disband, individual members commonly experience feelings of loss, and may set up reunions or alumni to share experiences and talk about the past. Generally, the greater difficulties and challenges that have faced a group, the more likely reunions are to endure over time (Moreland and Levine, 1989).

Cross-cultural considerations

Throughout the chapters that follow, space is devoted to consideration of how and whether very different cultures affect and change theory, findings and research on small groups. Most of the theory and research produced by social psychologists derives from western societies such as the United States of America, Great Britain and Australia/New Zealand. It is therefore entirely appropriate and correct to determine whether theory and research produced in such western societies generalises and holds true in other cultures, particularly eastern cultures. One of the key differences resulting from Hofstede's classic and ground-breaking research is the *individualism–collectivism dimension*. This dimension identifies a culture along a continuum where at the individualism extreme the culture is identified by individuals placing personal achievement over the group as a whole. Collectivism is where, for the individual, the group is more important than the person. Typically western countries are towards the individualism end and eastern cultures (such as China) towards the collectivism end of the dimension. We will return to this dimension when we consider cross-cultural differences in the chapters that follow.

Hofstede (1980) obtained information from over 100,000 individuals from 40 countries in his study. The primary method of research was to have a questionnaire completed which produced four dimensions on which cultures were shown to vary. These include the individualistic–collectivistic dimensions already mentioned, as well as the following:

- *power distance* — degree of respect and deference shown by subordinates to those in authority
- *uncertainty avoidance* — importance of forward planning and creation of stability in an individual's approach to life
- *masculinity–femininity* — emphasis on achievement (masculinity) or interpersonal harmony (femininity)

You may regard the label of the last dimension, masculinity-femininity, as unfortunate; however Hofstede did claim that this actually reflected male–female differences across cultures. Some of the findings for 10 of the countries sampled are given in Table 1.4.

TABLE 1.4 Rankings of 10 countries from the sample of 40 studied by Hofstede (1983)

Country	Power distance	Uncertainty avoidance	Individualism	Masculinity femininity
Australia	41	37	2	16
Germany	43	29	15	9
Great Britain	43	47	3	9
Greece	27	1	30	18
Hong Kong	15	49	37	18
Japan	33	7	22	1
Malaysia	1	46	36	25
Sweden	47	49	10	53
USA	38	43	1	15
Venezuela	5	21	50	3

Note:
The ranking is out of 80. A ranking of 1 indicates a strong emphasis on achievement.

As can be seen, Greeks obtained the ranking of 1 for uncertainty avoidance, meaning that the Greeks seemed least concerned about control and forward planning compared to individuals from countries such as Great Britain, Hong Kong, Sweden and the USA. With respect to individualism, Australia, Great Britain and the USA came out as the most individualistic cultures, while Hong King, Malaysia and Venezuela were the most collectivistic. Note also that on the basis of this research, Japan is the most achievement-oriented and Sweden the most concerned with interpersonal harmony. The dimensions of uncertainty avoidance and masculinity–femininity have produced less consistent results in subsequent research. The power distance and individualism–collectivism dimensions have endured and attracted a great deal of research since Hofstede's (1980) original research (Smith and Bond, 1998).

Organisation of this book

This book is focused on the behaviour of small groups, and has deliberately avoided looking at behaviour between groups. This means that theory and research concerned with social identity and intergroup relations is not considered here. There are many excellent texts that deal with this important area of social psychology (Augoustinos and Walker, 1995; Brown, 2000; Pennington, 2000). The following five chapters provide a full consideration of small group processes and how groups differ from individuals.

Chapter 2 considers issues to do with measurement of small group behaviour and ethical guidelines that need to be followed. Chapter 3 looks at how individuals behave and perform in small groups from two perspectives: individual performance in front of an audience, and in small groups where face-to-face interaction takes place. Chapter 4 looks at how groups develop over time and how groups are structured; in the latter cohesiveness, group norms, status and roles are all considered. Chapter 5 looks at co-operation, conflict and social influence in small groups. Chapter 6 takes a detailed look at theory and research on leadership including behavioural and personality approaches, leadership effectiveness, and gender and cultural influences on leadership. The final chapter, Chapter 7, compares individual and group decision-making, and ends by considering the question of whether or not the individual or group is best or which, if any, is more effective.

Summary

A small group may be regarded as a number of people interacting in some way with each other. This distinguishes it from an aggregate of people which is no more than a collection of unrelated individuals. Small groups may be formal or informal. The former tend to be created by organisations for a specific purpose, while the latter are people who come together because of a common interest, often for social or leisure reasons or as a self-help group.

Membership of a group may be formal or informal and be officially or unofficially based. People join formal groups because they are appointed or offer a particular expertise. Informal groups attract people more because joining provides security, enhances self-esteem and fulfils social needs more generally.

Communication in small groups may serve a number of different functions, including: conveying information or ideas; expressing and conveying feelings; motivating others, or controlling others. At times, communication may be facilitated or meet barriers. Small groups tend to develop a communication structure. Where structures are imposed from outside they are called communication networks. Types of networks include the wheel, chain, circle, and can be categorised as centralised or decentralised. Electronic communication facilitates faster communication between members of a group; the question to be answered is whether such communication results in groups operating and performing more effectively.

Small groups exist in a social and environmental context. This includes the physical, social and temporal environments. Differences between cultures need to be considered to ascertain whether theory and research findings are widely generalisable. The most influential dimensional difference between eastern and western cultures is that of collectivism–individualism respectively.

Further reading

Napier, R. W. and Gershenfeld, M. K. (1999) *Groups: Theory and Experience* (6th edn), Boston, MA: Houghton-Mifflin. A useful and accessible text which has chapters on communication, membership and group development which go into greater depth than this chapter. A detailed consideration is also given of self-help groups, total quality management and focus groups.

Smith, P. B. and Harris Bond, M. (1998) *Social Psychology Across Cultures* (2nd edn), London: Prentice-Hall. A highly respected and well-written text that draws together a vast array of theory and research in social psychology on cross-cultural differences.

Chapter 2

Measuring behaviour in small groups

Introduction

PAUSE FOR A MINUTE TO consider two small groups – one of which you are a member and one that you regularly come into contact with and are able to observe. These small groups may be work groups, groups of students or simply groups of friends. Think about the group you are a member of and the other individuals in the group. Does each person make an equal contribution? Does each person show a positive approach to the rest of the group? Do different people in the group make different contributions, for example, through specialist knowledge? Does the group work well together and achieve its goals? No doubt you can think of many other questions to ask about your group. The same questions can be asked about the other group, but since you are not a member of it you may have less insight and feel less confident in the answers you might give to the above and related questions.

A social psychologist faced with such questions would want to find evidence to support the answers that may be given. One way or another such evidence will be based on attempts to measure behaviour and perceptions/attitudes of the members of the group. In what follows we will look in some detail at the issues and challenges presented to social psychologists when attempting directly to observe group behaviour. We will then consider two well-developed and highly respected systems for measuring behaviour and/or perceptions. Both have been developed by Robert Bales, a highly influential social psychologist. These systems are *Interaction Process Analysis* (IPA) and *SYMLOG*. Finally, we will consider barriers and pitfalls that may face anybody attempting to observe and record group behaviour. This section deliberately does not cover research methods and data analysis procedures commonly employed by social psychologists. There are many texts devoted to these topics (see e.g. Breakwell *et al.*, 2000; Coolican, 1999).

Observation

It is simple to say that you want to base answers (or responses) to such questions as those given above on evidence derived from observation of interactions in the group. However, once you start thinking about what is involved and what decisions have to be made, observation becomes a very complex matter (Wilkinson, 2000).

Type of observer

The first decision to be made is whether you are going to observe the group you are a member of – and hence be a *participant observer* – or observe a group to which you do not belong. Participant observation has the advantage that you have additional insights into the group. This may help you gain better knowledge of the attitudes and beliefs of the other group members (and your own). However, the major drawbacks are that as a participant observer it is difficult to be objective, and you may know what the research is about and unduly influence the group. In addition, there are ethical issues that need to be considered; for example, are the other members of the group aware you are in a dual role? If not, should they be told? Section 2.5 looks more widely at ethical issues in research on small groups in social psychology. Finally, a participant observer has two roles – observer and contributor to the group. Doing both well may prove over-demanding, and it is likely that one of the roles may suffer at the expense of the other. Participant observation is usually to be avoided because of these drawbacks. However, sometimes it may be the only way to gain knowledge about a group; this is particularly true of religious cults, a group of political activists and so on, who would not permit observation by an outsider to take place.

'Live' or recorded observation?

The second decision to be made is whether observation of the group is going to be 'live' or recorded in some way so that analyses of behaviours can take place later and in a much less pressured way. Video-recording is usually to be preferred if possible and where the group, or organisation that the group belongs to, has given permission. However, placing cameras in front of a group or telling them that they are being video-recorded may change how they normally behave. Sometimes an acclimatisation period helps, but some people are just 'camera shy' or anxious from the knowledge that they are being recorded. Making observations of a group 'live', i.e. while the group is actually interacting, may result in more 'natural' behaviour. This may not be as 'natural' as not being observed at all, but there comes a point when social psychologists are not able easily to determine the effect of any type of observation on group behaviour. A group could be put on 'candid camera' – observed without their knowledge – but there are ethical constraints and ethical guidelines (see section 2.5) that would usually rule this out. Live observation demands a great deal of preparation on the part of the observer before the observation can take place. This preparation is needed for the analysis of a video-recording, with the difference that the video-recording can be played again and again, and hence analysed from a different or more refined perspective on repeated viewings. With live observation it all happens only once and is then gone!

Systematic observation

Almost all social psychological observations of groups are systematic, using standard procedures that the observers have been given training for and clearly defined categories of the behaviours that are to be observed. In the next section, when considering Bales' (1950) Interaction Process Analysis method, we will see how important these issues are. An example here may help clarify what is involved. Consider one of the groups you identified at the start of this section. Suppose you wish to know more about how each individual in the group reacts or behaves when something negative happens which presents a barrier to achieving the group goal. Clearly you can record what each person actually says, but you also need to capture how it is said. Somebody may make light of the problem but say it in such a way that it is clear the problem is viewed as insurmountable. Following from this, does one or more person in the group make positive contributions to help the group go forward and attempt to overcome the problem? If so, how is this done? Non-verbal behaviour plays an important role in group interaction, since in face-to-face group interaction, body posture, eye contact, whether the person is smiling or frowning, each have a strong and fairly immediate impact on others in the group. Observation of the behaviour of individuals in a small group therefore requires a clear definition of each behaviour to be observed, together with evidence that it can be reliably observed.

Reliability of observations

The *reliability* of observations is critical. This can be assessed in two ways. First, the same observer can analyse a video on two or more occasions for the same predefined categories of behaviour. If observations of the same behaviours are categorised in the same way on each occasion we can say that *intra-rater reliability* is high. That is, the same observer categorises the same behaviours at different times in the same way. The second way is to ask two or more observers to view the behaviour and categorise according to predefined definitions. If the same behaviours are categorised in the same or highly similar ways by the two or more observers we can say that *inter-rater reliability* is high. If either of these two approaches produces poor agreement about the categorising of behaviours, reliability is low. This has serious and often fatal consequences for the research, since if the evidence is unreliable, any answer to a research question will also be unreliable and usually worthless. Reliability of observation will often depend on how well the behaviours are defined and on the training given to observers before analysis of the 'real' group interaction takes place.

Clear, unambiguous definitions of behaviours are essential. It also has to be decided what behaviours to observe; given that it is usually not desirable or easy to observe everything that goes on in group interaction. Once definitions and categories of behaviours have been decided, decisions need to be made about whether just the recording of the occurrence of the behaviour will be enough or whether duration is also needed. In addition, some written comment or description of the behaviour is usually made by the researcher, since no two behaviours are identical and variations of similar behaviours may represent the same category of behaviour.

Sampling of behaviours

The type of sampling must also be decided upon. Basically there are two types: event sampling and time sampling. Event sampling means that every occurrence of the event or category of behaviour is recorded for the total period of group interaction. Time sampling means that selected periods of time of group interaction are selected; for example, a group may be observed for 10 minutes every half-hour. Time sampling is best used when the group interaction takes place over a long period of time, usually a day or more. If a group is together for only an hour or two, event sampling for the whole period is probably the optimum approach. Sometimes both types of sampling may be used at the same time.

A final consideration is the problem of *observer bias*. The problem here is particularly acute when the researcher observing and recording group behaviour is also aware of the purpose of the research or the question being asked. The categorisation of behaviours in a group setting is not clear-cut, and requires much preparation and training. Thus it may happen that the informed observer will categorise more ambiguous behaviours in certain ways to support the research hypothesis. The standard way around this is to use 'blind' observers; that is, observers who do not know what the research is about. In this way biased categorisation of behaviours will usually be avoided.

This completes our consideration of what is involved in observation of groups, and provides you with some insight into the large number of decisions the social psychologist needs to make when embarking on the analysis of group behaviour. The main issues covered are summarised in Table 2.1.

TABLE 2.1 Main issues that need to be considered when planning observations of group behaviour

Observation issue	Comment
Type of observation	Participant observer or outside of the group? Participant observer has more insight but less objective
Record observation or conduct live observation	Recording of group allows multiple observations, with 'live' observation only having one chance to analyse the behaviour
Systematic observations	Requires carefully pre-defined categories to observe and training of observers in these categories
Reliability	Two types are intra-rater and inter-rater. Both require same behaviours to be categorised in same way by same person or others for reliability to be high
Sampling	Need to decide whether to use event sampling or time sampling. Event sampling best for short observations of group interaction
Observer bias	Observers may bias behaviour categorisation to support research hypothesis. Best to use 'blind' observers, i.e. observers who do not know what research is about

Only very careful planning and consideration of these points will result in high-quality research, producing evidence that we can trust. We now move on to consider two systems for the analysis of groups.

Interaction Process Analysis

Perhaps the most well-developed, historically often used and widely tested observational technique for analysing group behaviour is the *Interaction Process Analysis* (IPA) method developed by Robert Bales about fifty years ago (Bales, 1950, 1953, 1970). IPA was designed specifically for the analysis of groups that come together to achieve a specific task; for example, work groups, project groups, juries, child abuse case conferences. However, the approach is equally applicable to more informal groups which do not have a specific task as their objective; for example, a group of friends or other types of social groups.

The IPA system developed by Bales assumes that all behaviours which occur in group interaction can be located in just 12 different categories. Before looking at these categories it is important to appreciate that Bales developed IPA from a functional theoretical perspective. Bales claimed that for a group to function effectively it must be able to solve two types of problems. First are task-related behaviours which help the group achieve its goal; if a group cannot find a solution for the behaviours needed to achieve the task or goal, it will fail. Second are socio-emotional behaviours which are concerned with finding approaches to interpersonal interaction between group members which foster positive feelings and behaviours needed for the group to want to work together. This is often referred to as the cohesiveness of a group (see Chapter 4). If the members of a group are unable to find ways of working together at an interpersonal level, the group will be characterised by conflict and will fail. This categorisation of group behaviours into task-related and socio-emotional is then broken down into two categories of each: socio-emotional positive, which help the group, and socio-emotional negative, which hinder the group from making progress. The task-related behaviours are broken down into the two categories of task-related questions and answers. This yields four categories, each of which has three components, as shown in Figure 2.1.

Two of the components from the task-related and socio-emotional categories are linked together. For example, components 5 and 8 are linked by (b) which represents problems that group members are having with evaluation of matters to do with the task. Components 2 and 11 are linked by (e) which represents socio-emotional or interpersonal problems that members of the group are

Main categories		Components	Component links
Socio-emotional area: positive	1	**Shows solidarity:** raises other's status, gives help, rewards	
	2	**Shows tension release:** jokes, laughs, shows satisfaction	
	3	**Agrees:** shows passive acceptance, understands, concurs, complies	
Task area: attempted answers	4	**Gives suggestion:** direction, implying autonomy for other	
	5	**Gives opinion:** evaluation, analysis, expresses feeling, wish	
	6	**Gives orientation:** information, repeats, clarifies, conforms	
Task area: questions	7	**Asks for orientation:** information, repetition, confirmation	a b c d e f
	8	**Asks for opinion:** evaluation, analysis, expression of feeling	
	9	**Asks for suggestion:** direction, possible ways of action	
Socio-emotional area: negative	10	**Disagrees:** shows passive rejection, formality, withholds help	
	11	**Shows tensions:** asks for help, withdraws out of field	
	12	**Shows antagonism:** deflates other's status, defends or asserts self	

Key to component links
(a) problems of communication
(b) problems of evaluation
(c) problems of control
(d) problems of decision
(e) problems of tension reduction
(f) problems of reintegration

FIGURE 2.1 Bales' Interaction Process Analysis showing links between components

Source: adapted from Bales (1950)

having with how to reduce and deal with tension in the group when it arises.

Bales required that observers who wish to use IPA go through between three and four months of intensive training in order to achieve an acceptably high level of reliability (see section 2.3). Research on the reliability of IPA has shown good reliability both between different observers and for the same observer at different times. Bales trained observers to use a device with 12 buttons on it which recorded results on moving paper. An appropriate button was pressed when the observer wished to record one of the 12 components shown in Figure 2.1. Clearly, computers have supplanted this recording device; however, whichever approach is used, Bales was able to obtain both recordings of the categories of behaviour of the group and how they varied over time. For example, Bales found that when the group initially came together, orientation behaviours (6 and 7 in Figure 2.1) were strongly present. This was often followed by a phase of evaluation (5 and 8 in Figure 2.1), and then a period of control (4 and 9 in Figure 2.1).

Bales (1955) analysed 24 groups in 96 different sessions and produced over 71,000 IPA observations. This gave a profile that is typical of many small groups (see Table 2.2). From this it may be seen that over 30 per cent of behaviours by group members have to do with giving opinions, while only a small percentage have to do with asking for suggestions, showing both solidarity and antagonism.

TABLE 2.2 Profile of group behaviour using IPA. Notice the high percentage of task answers and positive socio-emotional behaviours shown by the groups

Interaction Process Analysis			Percentage	
			Component	Category
Socio-emotional positive	1	Shows solidarity	3.4	
	2	Shows tension release	6.0	25.9
	3	Shows agreement	16.5	
Task answers	4	Gives suggestion	8.0	
	5	Gives opinion	30.1	56.0
	6	Gives information	17.9	
Task questions	7	Asks for information	3.5	
	8	Asks for opinion	2.4	7.0
	9	Asks for suggestion	1.1	
Socio-emotional negative	10	Shows disagreement	7.8	
	11	Shows tensions	2.7	11.2
	12	Shows antagonism	0.7	

Source: adapted from Bales (1955)

Some of the key findings about group behaviour to arise from the use of IPA are that: two leaders may emerge (a task leader and a socio-emotional leader); the person who talks the most receives the greatest attention from other group members; the larger the group, the more likely one person is to dominate; and most behaviours are related to task categories on IPA.

IPA is a powerful tool to be used by researchers observing the behaviour of members of a group. However, IPA ignores completely the views of the group members themselves. Bales' focus on objective, observer measurement fails to recognise the importance of what each of the group members actually think and feel. The development of SYMLOG by Bales attempts to rectify this shortcoming. In addition, because the SYMLOG dimensions underlie the 12 IPA categories (Bales, 1970), SYMLOG can be seen to supersede IPA.

SYMLOG

SYMLOG is an acronym for a *SY*stem for the *M*ultiple *L*evel *O*bservation of *G*roups, and provides a method for the study of small groups based upon measures taken from each individual in the group. Unlike IPA, SYMLOG has been designed for a wider range of groups such as families, project teams and groups of students in education (Bales and Cohen, 1979). SYMLOG offers a number of different methods for the observation of groups as well, including actual recording and categorising of behaviour. Here we will focus on the Adjective Rating Form (ARF) and how this gives a profile of the group based upon the perceptions of each individual member of the group.

The ARF is based on three dimensions used to describe a group. These are:

- dominant–submissive (Up–Down)
- instrumentally controlled–emotionally expressive (Forward–Backward)
- friendly–unfriendly (Positive–Negative).

Note that the dimensions (such as Up–Down) are named for dimensions in a 'real' three-dimensional space. SYMLOG is a field theory; that is, the dimensions are not purely abstractions, but social interaction is said to take place in a three-dimensional arena.

The dominant–submissive dimension concerns whether a group member is active, talks a lot and is purposeful, or looks to others, and is obedient, passive and says little. The instrumentally controlled–emotionally expressive dimension concerns whether a group member is task-oriented (problem-solving, hard-

Your Name _____ Group _____

Name of person described _____ Circle the best choice for each item

		(0)	(1)	(2)	(3)	(4)
U	... active, dominant, talks a lot	... never	... rarely	... sometimes	... often	... always
UP	... extroverted, outgoing, positive	... never	... rarely	... sometimes	... often	... always
UPF	... a purposeful democratic task leader	... never	... rarely	... sometimes	... often	... always
UF	... an assertive business-like manager	... never	... rarely	... sometimes	... often	... always
UNF	... authoritarian, controlling, disapproving	... never	... rarely	... sometimes	... often	... always
UN	... domineering, tough-minded, powerful	... never	... rarely	... sometimes	... often	... always
UNB	... provocative, egocentric, shows off	... never	... rarely	... sometimes	... often	... always
UB	... jokes around, expressive, dramatic	... never	... rarely	... sometimes	... often	... always
UPB	... entertaining, sociable, smiling, warm	... never	... rarely	... sometimes	... often	... always
P	... friendly, equalitarian	... never	... rarely	... sometimes	... often	... always
PF	... works co-operatively with others	... never	... rarely	... sometimes	... often	... always
F	... analytical, task-oriented, problem-solving	... never	... rarely	... sometimes	... often	... always
NF	... legalistic, has to be right	... never	... rarely	... sometimes	... often	... always
N	... unfriendly, negativistic	... never	... rarely	... sometimes	... often	... always
NB	... irritable, cynical, won't co-operate	... never	... rarely	... sometimes	... often	... always
B	... shows feelings and emotion	... never	... rarely	... sometimes	... often	... always
PB	... affectionate, likeable, fun to be with	... never	... rarely	... sometimes	... often	... always
DP	... looks up to others, appreciative, trusful	... never	... rarely	... sometimes	... often	... always
DPF	... gentle, willing to accept responsibility	... never	... rarely	... sometimes	... often	... always
DF	... obedient, works submissively	... never	... rarely	... sometimes	... often	... always
DNF	... self-punishing, works too hard	... never	... rarely	... sometimes	... often	... always
DN	... depressed, sad, resentful, rejecting	... never	... rarely	... sometimes	... often	... always
DNB	... alienated, quits, withdraws	... never	... rarely	... sometimes	... often	... always
DB	... afraid to try, doubts own ability	... never	... rarely	... sometimes	... often	... always
DPB	... quietly happy just to be with others	... never	... rarely	... sometimes	... often	... always
D	... passive, introverted, says little	... never	... rarely	... sometimes	... often	... always

Key

U – dominant	D – submissive
P – friendly	N – unfriendly
F – task controlled	B – emotionally expressive

FIGURE 2.2   The Adjective Rating Form (ARF) used by Bales

Source: from Bales and Cohen © 1979 by The Free Press

working, authoritarian) or more concerned with showing feelings and emotions, concerned with how others feel. The friendly–unfriendly dimension concerns friendly or unfriendly behaviours shown by the group members in interaction with others. Each of these bipolar dimensions has three components, thus yielding 27 separate rating items on the ARF. This is shown in Figure 2.2.

Using the ARF, *each* member of the group rates all other group members separately; this includes ratings of the self and may also include abstractions such as 'how you wished you had behaved'. Once this is done, the 5-point rating scale is used to calculate one score for each of the three main dimensions. To do this, taking the dominant–submissive dimension as an example, calculate the score for the dominant end by adding up each rating score in Figure 2.2 that has a U on the left-hand side. Then add up the score for each rating scale that has a D on the left-hand side for the submissive end. The range for each is 0 to 36. Suppose in rating yourself you get 25 for dominant and 10 for submissive. Take away one from the other; this yields 15, and since the dominant score is higher this is a score of 15 in the dominant end of this dimension. This is then done in a similar way for the other two dimensions. Let us suppose you have done this for a three-person group of which you are a member. The results are as shown in Table 2.3.

TABLE 2.3 Imaginary ratings for a three-person group on each of the three SYMLOG dimensions

Group member	Instrumentally controlled – emotionally expressive		Friendly – unfriendly		Dominant – submissive	
Self	5	Instrumentally controlled	20	Friendly	15	Dominant
Linda	10	Emotionally expressive	10	Unfriendly	5	Dominant
John	15	Instrumentally controlled	5	Friendly	10	Submissive

This shows that you regard yourself to be slightly on the task-oriented side (5), very friendly (20) and quite dominant (15). By contrast, you perceive John to be very task-oriented (15), mildly friendly (5) and quite emotionally expressive (10). You perceive Linda to be quite unfriendly (10).

The final step is to provide an average for the group, based upon the three individual scores in this case. For example, the average task–social score for self would be the average of how you were rated on the task–social by Linda, John and yourself. These averages present a profile for the group. Suppose that for our imaginary three-person group the averages were as follows:

Self	15F	(task)	10P	(friendly)	20U	(dominant)
Linda	15B	(emotion)	15N	(unfriendly)	5U	(dominant)
John	10F	(task)	15P	(friendly)	15D	(submissive)

You would see from this profile that Linda is seen as being unfriendly, emotionally expressive and slightly dominant. You are seen as task-oriented, dominant and friendly, and John is seen as task-oriented, friendly and submissive. Based on this profile, how well do you think the group would work together? You might infer that a lot would be left to you because of John's submissiveness and Linda's unfriendliness. Moving the group forward might be quite stressful for you!

This outline of one of the methods offered by SYMLOG serves to demonstrate how much work is involved in attempting to measure group behaviour by using a well-developed and sophisticated set of tools. Clearly, SYMLOG requires users to be highly trained and knowledgeable about its scoring and analysis methods. It is a very powerful tool for measuring group behaviour from the perspective of the perceptions of the individual group members.

The two approaches to measuring group behaviour provide complementary methods, since IPA is used by observers of group interaction and SYMLOG by the actual group members themselves. You may wish to try out each of these methods for yourself. This is to be recommended, since only by using these tools will you gain insight into issues and problems to do with measurement (but remember: proper use has to be by trained psychologists).

Bales has made an enormous contribution to both the theory of and research into groups. It is to his great credit that Interaction Process Analysis and SYMLOG are still widely regarded by social psychologists as the most well-developed and dependable methods to use. They are a little complicated, and demand training and extensive usage before a researcher can apply them and use the findings with confidence.

Ethical considerations

Whether you are conducting a small-scale project in social psychology as part of your coursework or you are a well-qualified, experienced and highly regarded psychologist, all research must adhere to and comply with ethical guidelines. The British Psychological Society (1998) has published a booklet entitled *Code of Conduct, Ethical Principles and Guidelines*. We have already come across some ethical issues when considering observational issues in section 2.2. In what follows we will look at consent, deception, debriefing, confidentiality and withdrawal as ethical issues to consider when planning or conducting research on small groups.

Consent

The British Psychological Society booklet states that 'psychologists shall normally carry out investigations or interventions only with the valid consent of participants' (p.2). Notice that the important words here are 'normally' and 'valid consent'. The use of 'normally' does allow psychologists to conduct research without full *consent* of participants, but this should be avoided wherever possible. However, when observing behaviour in small groups it may sometimes affect how individuals behave if full information is given about the research to gain valid consent. For example, suppose you were interested in patterns of non-verbal communication between group members. Informing them of this to gain valid consent may affect their non-verbal behaviour. In such cases psychologists may be vague about the purpose of the research, but must fully debrief participants afterwards. Valid consent then is a stringent requirement where full information of the research should be provided to the participant.

Deception

Deception of participants is a major ethical concern for psychologists. Clearly, deception should be avoided wherever possible. However, the British Psychological Society recognises that 'the statement of the research hypothesis in advance of the collection of data would make much psychological research impossible' (p.5). You will see in Chapter 5 when we come to consider Asch's (1956) studies on conformity that one participant in a small group was not aware that the others in the group were under instruction from Asch to behave in certain ways. In effect, the participant was deceived into thinking that the others in the group were 'real' participants just like him- or herself.

Debriefing

Where participants have not been fully informed of the nature of the research or have been deceived, it is incumbent upon psychologists to *debrief* the participants. Debriefing is where the researcher explains to the participant what the research is about. When debriefing, the researcher should also ask the participant if he or she had any concerns or worries about what they had just participated in. If so, the researcher should reassure the participant and do their best to allow the participant to leave in a comfortable frame of mind. One of the main objectives of debriefing is to try to ensure that the participants leave, after having been part of the research, in as similar a state as possible as when they entered the research. This is especially important if the research has caused a degree of personal upset or, for example, induced a negative mood state.

Right to withdraw

Before taking part in the research, participants should be informed of their *right to withdraw* at any stage. When conducting research on small groups it is to be hoped that none of the group members will withdraw, since this may mean the whole group has to be abandoned. However, the researcher must respect the right of an individual to withdraw and simply accept the consequences. With small groups, another group composed of entirely new participants might have to be substituted for the group that had to be abandoned.

Confidentiality

Finally, data provided by participants should be *confidential* and presented anonymously (so that participants cannot be identified). The guidelines put this more clearly and explicitly: 'Psychologists . . . shall take all reasonable steps to preserve the confidentiality of information acquired through their practice or research and to protect the privacy of individuals or organisations about whom information is collected or held' (p.3). This may be particularly important where video- or audio-recordings of small groups, such as child abuse case conferences, are made. The recordings and data must also be held in a secure place to ensure access is limited only to the researchers. The Data Protection Act 1998 allows participants to have access to data derived from their participation in research, should it be requested.

   The adherence to stringent ethical guidelines in the conduct of research on small groups requires a great deal of planning and careful thought before undertaking the research. This is required of all research, and of all those conducting research, from the student to the professor.

Summary

Observation of small group behaviour requires decisions to be made about type of observer, 'live' or recorded observation, systematic observation, and how reliability within and between observers is to be established. The types of behaviours to sample also need to be decided upon.

Interaction Process Analysis was developed by Robert Bales for observers to analyse small group behaviour. All behaviours in group interaction are allocated to one of four main categories: socio-emotional positive and negative, and task-related questions and answers. IPA does not attempt to take into account the views and attitudes of each group member. SYMLOG stands for a system for the multiple level observation of groups. It provides a measure of small groups based upon measures taken from each individual in the group. Three dimensions are used to describe each group member and the profile of the whole group: dominant–submissive, instrumentally controlled–emotionally expressive, and friendly–unfriendly.

All research conducted on small groups must conform to a set of guidelines set by a country's professional body in psychology. Ethical considerations need to be given to participant consent, deception of participants, debriefing, right to withdrawal and confidentiality. These guidelines apply to all psychologists, student or professor, conducting psychological research.

Further reading

Breakwell, G. M., Hammond, S. and Fife-Shaw, C. (eds) (2000) *Research Methods in Psychology* (2nd edn), London: Sage. A well-regarded text with individual chapters written by specialists in their field. Has a good chapter on direct observation, as well as useful chapters on focus groups, ethnographic and action research and interviewing, which are relevant to small group research.

BPS (1998) *Code of Conduct, Ethical Principles and Guidelines*, Leicester: The British Psychological Society. This 45-page booklet provides comprehensive guidelines for a code of conduct for psychologists and psychological research. It is available from The British Psychological Society, St Andrew's House, 48 Princess Road East, Leicester LE1 7DR; or visit the website at *www.bps.org.uk/about/rules.cfm*

Individuals
and groups

Introduction

I NDIVIDUALS INTERACT AND RELATE to others in a group in
many ways. We normally think of face-to-face interaction and
verbal communication as the most common and normal mode of
individual interaction in groups. However, it is well known that
groups bring something to a task or problem which is superior
to the contribution of any one individual. The focus of this chapter
is on how individuals behave and perform in small groups. This
will be looked at from two main perspectives. First, when individuals perform in front of an audience where there is little or
no communication with the observing group or audience. Second,
how individuals perform in small groups where face-to-face interaction and communication takes place. The former relates to a
large body of theory and research in social psychology on social
facilitation. The latter includes social loafing and the problem-
solving technique of brainstorming. How individuals behave and
perform in small groups is taken up in other chapters, most
notably Chapter 7 on decision-making. In the following, the

assumptions that individual performance is enhanced in a group setting and that groups perform better than individuals is both considered and questioned.

Alone or in groups?

Given a choice, would you prefer to work on a task alone or with a group of people? On the surface this seems a simple question, but when investigated by social psychologists the answer is quite complicated and depends on a number of factors.

Vancouver and Ilgen (1989) speculated that one important variable would be the nature of the task itself, and investigated how males and females responded to the offer of working alone or with another person on sex-congruent and sex-incongruent tasks. Sex-congruent tasks were conceptualised as tasks typically associated with males or females and with which most of one sex would be familiar. For example, in line with stereotypes, a sex-congruent task for a male might be repairing a car and for a female sewing an item of clothing. Sex-incongruent tasks are those associated with the opposite sex. Vancover and Ilgen (1989) used equally difficult tasks that had earlier been established as masculine (building a shed) or feminine (designing a shop-window). They then presented men and women with both types of task and asked participants if they preferred to work alone or with another person on each of the tasks. As Figure 3.1 shows, men preferred to work alone more on sex-congruent tasks and with another person on sex-incongruent tasks. Women showed greater preferences than men, as shown in Figure 3.1, in that they quite strongly preferred to work with a partner on a sex-incongruent task and alone on a sex-congruent task.

These findings may also reflect stereotypical images that are held of men and women: men feel they should be able to do things on their own, whereas women are more sociable and may prefer to work in collaboration with others. However, Vancouver and Ilgen found no relationship between the affiliative needs of males and females and their wish to work with another person. The

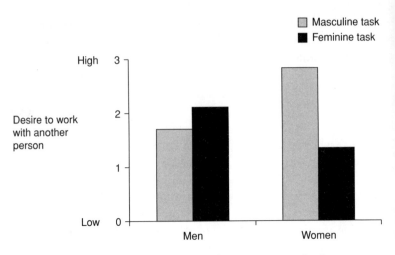

FIGURE 3.1 Preference of men and women to work alone or with another person on sex-congruent or sex-incongruent tasks

Source: adapted from Vancouver and Ilgen (1989)

picture that emerges, therefore, is quite complicated, and shows that the desire to want to work with another person may be determined by sex of the person, type of task, experience of doing a similar task before, and need for social interaction. The study clearly demonstrates that both men and women have a general desire to work with other people, regardless of the type of task. Figure 3.1 quite clearly shows that while sex and type of task make a difference, the desire to work with others is prevalent across all conditions of the experiment.

Working with other people may provide reassurance, help produce better solutions to a problem, generate a greater range of ideas, bolster confidence when faced with a new task that we have no experience of, and generally be enjoyable because of the rewards other people provide. We shall pick up some of these issues when we come to consider the technique of *brainstorming* later in this chapter (see section 3.5). We now consider how well individuals perform a task in the presence of other people.

Social facilitation

Imagine you have been playing the flute for over ten years and that you are soon to play in front of a large audience. Do you think your performance will be enhanced or worsened compared to when you have played alone when practising the music? Now imagine that you have been asked to play tennis in front of a large group of people and that you have hardly played tennis before, let alone received any coaching. You decide to have a short practice with a friend. Do you think your performance at tennis will be better or worse in front of an audience than when you practised without an audience present? These are questions that the area of *social facilitation* in social psychology has been investigating for over 100 years.

Performance in the presence of others

The first psychologist formally to investigate social facilitation was Triplett (1898), who noticed that racing cyclists travelled faster on a racing circuit when in competition with another cyclist compared with when cycling alone. Triplett (1898) conducted an experiment with young children who were asked to wind fishing line using a reel as fast as they could. In one of the experimental conditions each child wound the line alone, and in the other condition a child wound a line with another child present performing the same task. Triplett did not instruct the children in the latter condition to compete with each other. As predicted, children doing this task alone were slower than when together.

Some 20 years later, Gordon Allport, a founding father of modern experimental social psychology, was interested to discover how the mere presence of other people affected performance. Allport (1920) investigated a wide range of tasks from motor performance-type tasks (such as those of Triplett) to more psychological or cognitive tasks (such as word associations or more complex tasks such as generating arguments to disprove a statement). For both of these psychological tasks Allport (1920) reported social facilitation; that is, enhanced performance with other people present. Note that individuals performing tasks are doing so in the mere presence of others; no interaction or communication takes place with the audience. Studying individual performance in such conditions is an example of *co-action* in front of a passive (non-interacting) audience as opposed to *interaction*, which is perhaps more akin to how we normally think of small group behaviour. With interaction, people in a group are talking, working together and communicating in many different ways with other group members to perform a task collectively (subsequent chapters in this book look at the many different aspects of this type of small group behaviour).

Evidence for social facilitation has also been found among the non-human animal world. For example, rats eat faster when in a cage with other rats, ants in a sand-box dig more when with other ants, and pairs of rats copulate more when surrounded by other rats. In a study of human eating behaviour, de Castro and Brewer (1991) asked people to keep diaries of what they had eaten over a one-week period. When the diaries were analysed they found that people ate more fattening and larger meals when other people were present, although not necessarily eating together at the same table, than when eating alone.

All the evidence we have looked at so far points to the idea that the mere presence of others facilitates performance or enhances behaviour. Consider the two examples of flute playing and tennis playing given earlier. You may be surprised to learn that the presence of others is most likely to enhance your flute playing but to make your already poor tennis skills even worse. In many aspects of human behaviour, performance deteriorates in front of other people compared to when carried out alone.

The seemingly inconsistent effect of audiences on human behaviour was focused on by Zajonc (1965), who gave an explanation based on the idea that the presence of other people causes the individual to be aroused. He developed this into *drive theory*. This explanation has withstood the test of time, although other explanations have been developed, as we shall see.

Drive theory of social facilitation

Zajonc (1965) suggested that we find the mere presence of other people emotionally arousing. He then went on to make a fundamentally important distinction between *dominant* or accessible responses and *non-dominant* or inaccessible responses. Dominant or accessible responses are those we have learned, rehearsed or had considerable past experience of. In the examples given earlier, playing the flute would be regarded as a dominant response – you are practised, experienced and skilled at the task. Non-dominant or inaccessible responses are those that are not well learned and we have little experience of, such as the example of playing tennis.

Zajonc's drive theory claims that the mere presence of an audience is arousing, and that this increases the tendency to produce dominant responses. If the dominant responses are appropriate or correct in relation to the task, performance will be enhanced, but if inappropriate, performance will be impaired compared to when the person performs the task alone. This is shown in Figure 3.2.

This means that tasks we are skilled at, which are well learned and of which we have a long history of experience are likely to be enhanced in front of an audience. In contrast, tasks at which we are not skilled or those in the early stages of learning will be performed even more poorly in front of an audience. Take the example of teaching; Zajonc's drive theory predicts that an experienced, skilled teacher will do well in front of a class. In contrast, a new teacher may practise and rehearse at home and be satisfied with his or her performance. However, when the new teacher has to stand in front of a class he or she is likely to perform poorly, both according to his or her own expectations and to those of the students in the class.

While Zajonc's drive theory explanation is still regarded as valid, there are certain important questions it does not answer. Most noticeably is: Why should the presence of other people cause an individual to feel arousal in the first place? We will look at two explanations offered in answer to this question: evaluation apprehension and distraction–conflict theory.

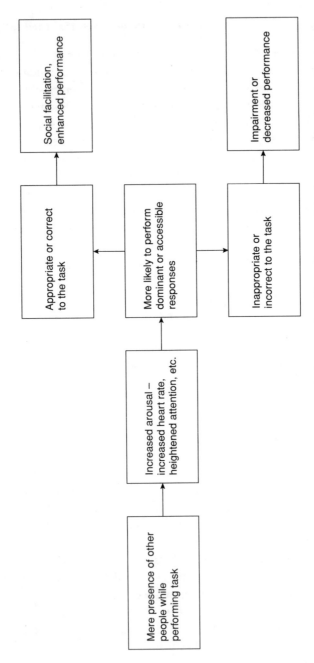

FIGURE 3.2 Drive theory of social facilitation showing the effect of arousal to increase dominant responses that may or may not be appropriate to the task

Source: adapted from Zajonc (1965)

Evaluation apprehension

Why should an audience arouse us? Cottrell (1972) suggested that performing in front of other people raises concerns about how we will be evaluated by those observing what we are doing. Concern about how other people will evaluate our performance makes us apprehensive, with the consequence that this causes *evaluation apprehension*, which is arousing. For this explanation of social facilitation to work we should find that the presence of others, even when they are not paying particular attention to individual performance, should cause evaluation apprehension. This is so since it is the individual's concern that he or she *may* be evaluated, rather than really being evaluated, which is of importance. Schmitt *et al.* (1986) provided evidence for this in an experiment where participants were required to type their own name over and over again. In one condition, the audience wore blindfolds and earphones with music playing; in another condition, the audience simply observed without blindfolds or earphones. Compared to working alone, participants in both audience conditions showed improved performance, but more so in the latter condition.

Other findings have also supported the evaluation apprehension explanation. For example, Seta and Seta (1992) found social facilitation effects to be greater when a high-status group of people who mattered to the individual were present, and less noticeable when the people present did not matter so much to the individual. Geen and Gange (1983) demonstrated individual differences where those who were less concerned about other people's evaluations showed less social facilitation than individuals who were highly concerned about how other people evaluated them. Generally, then, a sizeable body of evidence supports the idea that the mere presence of other people causes evaluation apprehension. However, this is not the whole story. Consider times when you have been in front of an audience: you may feel apprehensive, but you may also find the presence of other people distracting.

Distraction–conflict explanation

Performing in front of an audience, regardless of whether we think the audience is evaluating our behaviour, may simply be distracting because our attention is divided between the task at hand and observing the reactions of people in the audience. *Distraction–conflict theory* (Baron, 1986; Sanders, 1983) states that the presence of others causes our attention to be divided between the task at hand and people in the audience. In effect, the audience acts as a distractor. Conflict then arises for the individual as to whether to pay attention to the task or to the audience. When the task is simple or well learned the distraction does not affect performance and arousal causes social facilitation. By contrast where the task is novel or poorly learned, distraction effects are great and performance is impaired. This is because high conflict is caused by not knowing whether to pay attention to the task or the audience; this in turn leads to high levels of arousal that have an impairing effect on a non-dominant or inaccessible response.

Plenty of empirical evidence supports this explanation of social facilitation. For example, Sanders (1983) found that individuals who have little reason to pay attention to others, for example, when those others are performing other tasks themselves, show less social facilitation on a dominant response than when they have good reasons for paying attention to the audience. Other research has used non-human distractors such as bells or other noises and found social facilitation for dominant responses when distracting noises are present (Pessin, 1933).

Competing or complementary explanations?

We have considered three explanations of social facilitation: drive theory (Zajonc, 1965), evaluation apprehension (Cottrell, 1972), and distraction–conflict (Baron, 1986). Are these competing or complementary explanations? Figure 3.3 shows how the latter two explanations are related to showing how arousal occurs in the first place, while drive theory then takes over to explain social facilitation. The three explanations can therefore be seen as part of a wider model.

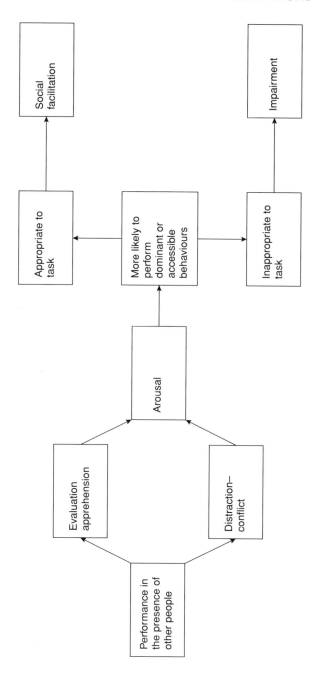

FIGURE 3.3 The role of evaluation apprehension and distraction–conflict in producing arousal resulting in increased likelihood of performing dominant tasks in front of an audience

Social loafing

We have looked at how individual performance is affected when one is behaving in the presence of other people, with either social facilitation or impairment being a consequence. The other side of the coin is to ask how individual performance is affected when one is working as part of a small group or team. In many group or team situations, individuals are working with others on a task where each individual contribution is added together to form a group product. Such tasks are known as *additive tasks* which range from, for example, a team of bricklayers working on the same building, a team of six rowers in a boat, a tug-of-war team, to a restaurant kitchen with a number of cooks. The common wisdom is that 'many hands make light work' (the proverb 'too many cooks spoil the broth' may also come to mind). You may have personal experience of working on a project with four or five other students and been frustrated that one person does not pull their weight. This latter problem captures the phenomenon of *social loafing*.

Conditions for social loafing

Social loafing was first studied by a French engineer called Ringlemann as early as 1913 (Kravitz and Martin, 1986). Ringlemann measured the combined effort of different-sized groups who were asked to pull a rope attached to a dynamometer. This measured the total force exerted. Ringlemann also measured the average force of each individual involved in the experiment. As you can see from Figure 3.4, as group size increased, the less force or effort was made by each individual in the group. This was originally called the *Ringlemann effect*. It is now known as social loafing because of the wide range of situations in which the phenomenon occurs.

Latané *et al.* (1979) conducted a number of different experiments – for example, asking participants to clap hands and cheer – and demonstrated the generality of social loafing. Subsequent research has shown social loafing to occur equally with males and

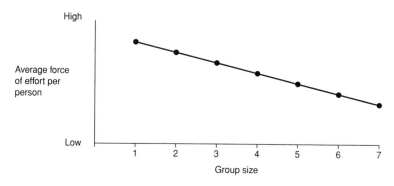

FIGURE 3.4 Average effort per person at pulling a rope as a function of group size. Reflection of the findings of Ringlemann

females, both for cognitive tasks as well as those involving physical effort, and across different cultures – although stronger in western cultures (Williams and Karau, 1991; Yamaguchi *et al.*, 1985). Hence it seems that, whenever people work together in small groups on an additive task, social loafing is likely to be present.

Two explanations of social loafing each offer a good account of the phenomenon: *social impact theory* (Latané and Nida, 1980) and the *collective effort model* (Karau and Williams, 1993). We will look briefly at each and compare them.

Social impact theory states that as group size increases the social force or impact on each individual member decreases. For example, consider a situation where you are working with two other students on a project that is assessed and contributes to your coursework. Your teacher or supervisor tells you to work hard, and gives you deadlines for each stage of the project and a final completion date. You feel the teacher has a strong impact on you and you work hard with the others on the project. Now imagine that you are in a group of 10 people working on the project. Social impact theory states that the impact of the teacher's instructions on this larger group will be much less. Each individual may feel less responsible or think his or her contribution to the project as a whole is not very important. The consequence of social impact theory being less for each individual as group size increases is a greater tendency for social loafing. One of the main shortcomings

57

of this explanation is that it does not really take account of the motivation and expectations the individual has when working on a specific task in a small group. Another shortcoming is that it assumes social loafing to exist in all small groups when this may not be the case.

The *collective effort model* (Karau and Williams, 1993) offers a comprehensive explanation of social loafing and indicates when it might and might not occur. This model states that when an individual is working with others on a task certain links are weakened, as follows:

- the link between individual effort and group performance or outcome is less obvious as group size increases;
- the link between group performance or outcome and the rewards an individual receives is less strong as group size increases.

The collective effort model also takes into account the motivation of an individual and further states that an individual will work hard at a task under the following conditions:

- the individual believes or expects his or her own efforts to result in better performance of the group product as a whole;
- the individual believes that individual effort will be recognised and rewarded;
- the rewards the individual will receive are ones valued and desired by the individual.

These general conditions should allow predictions to be made about when social loafing is most and least likely to occur. It is to this that we now turn.

Overcoming social loafing

The collective effort model predicts that social loafing will be less in evidence when: individuals in the group find the task to be interesting or important to them; when people work with friends or colleagues whom they respect; when their individual contribution is seen as unique or directly related to the outcome; and when an individual expects others in the group not to work well on the task. Karau and Williams (1993) conducted an analysis of nearly 50 published studies on social loafing and found good evidence for the above predictions, hence supporting the collective effort model. From this one would expect that techniques such as making the effort and work of each individual directly related and identifiable with the final group product should reduce social loafing. This may be achieved by breaking down the task into separate components and allocating an individual to work on one component. However, in many additive tasks this may not be possible – it is difficult to see how different subtasks can be allocated to a tug-of-war team. Other techniques include making the task seem more important to each individual, making the group more cohesive or feeling together as a group, and providing individual rather than group rewards for effort. Finally, punishment can be effective: setting a minimum standard of performance for a group, then punishing each person if the standard is not achieved may be effective (Miles and Greenberg, 1995). However, this may also result in the group not operating above the minimum standard set either!

Social compensation

From the account of social loafing given so far, you may think that all members of a group will exhibit the phenomenon. However, from your own personal experience of working in groups what is more often the case is that some work hard and others – or a sole individual – may not pull his or her weight at all. In some circumstances a *free-rider effect* may occur; this is where someone attaches themselves to a group, loafs or does little work, and picks up the rewards of the group outcomes (Kerr, 1983). The opposite of this is where an individual thinks that others in the group are leaving him or her to get on with all the work while they do little. The individual in this situation may then not be willing to exert full effort or work as hard as possible because of being taken for a 'sucker'. This has been called the *sucker effect* (Van Dijt and Wilke, 1993).

However, and by contrast, in some situations an individual may work extra hard to compensate for the performance of others in the group. This is known as *social compensation*, and is most likely to occur when an individual thinks that other group members are less able or willing to put in the effort on a task that is important to him or her. Williams and Karau (1991) produced evidence for this in a series of experiments. They found that when students expected their partner in a two-person group to perform poorly on a task involving generating novel ideas for the use of a knife, social compensation was found. This only happened when the experimenter made the task seem important and of value to the students by, for example, indicating that performance was evidence of high intelligence. Social compensation was found both when students expected their partner to make little effort or to have little ability for the task.

In summary, social loafing is a pervasive phenomenon that occurs in small groups working on additive tasks. However, under certain circumstances social loafing may be reduced or social compensation will occur. Social loafing is less likely to occur when individuals in a group are performing tasks of importance and value to them and can see direct links between effort and the group outcome.

Brainstorming

It is commonly accepted wisdom that a group of people are more likely to come up with a successful solution or new, creative ideas to a problem than an individual working alone. When faced with a problem to solve or finding unusual uses for something, people will often say 'let's brainstorm the problem'. The term 'brainstorm' has entered everyday language but will be used more formally in a company setting and informally in, say, student project work groups. Osborn (1957) introduced the technique and procedure of *brainstorming* for use in business and industry as a way of facilitating groups to be more creative, and to get out of routine and often rather boring ways of thinking. In this section we will first detail the procedure for brainstorming and then question how effective it really is compared to individual performance.

TABLE 3.1 Rules for the proper use of the brainstorming technique. Note that (5) is of fundamental importance

Key rules for brainstorming technique
1 Set a time limit for the brainstorming session – up to 30 minutes is normal.
2 One person needs to agree to act as the recorder, to write down ideas generated.
3 Each individual should offer ideas that come to mind with no discussion, comment or detail.
4 Individuals should not attempt to hold back any ideas they have.
5 Avoid any criticism of your own or other people's ideas.
6 Build on other people's ideas wherever possible.
7 Encourage or ensure that each person in the group is able to contribute equally.
8 A practice session, using a different problem, helps to ensure the above rules are followed.

The technique of brainstorming

Brainstorming is a technique designed to encourage small groups, formal or informal, to produce as many novel and creative ideas as possible. The idea is that individuals add and build on ideas suggested by other group members and do not make criticism or any evaluative comments during the brainstorming stage itself. Table 3.1 summarises the key rules that the whole group should properly abide by to brainstorm a problem.

The advantages of brainstorming are that the individuals in the group tend to find the experience enjoyable and stimulating; it encourages the sharing of ideas with others in the group; it reduces dependency on a single authority figure; and it encourages each person in the group to interact and participate. Generally, groups using the brainstorming technique believe it will result in the generation of more ideas and greater creativity compared to, for example, an individual working alone. However, a sizeable body of research questions the validity of these claims and suggests that brainstorming may be a poor way for groups to approach a task and problem-solve.

Effectiveness of brainstorming

The effectiveness of brainstorming to improve the quality of creative ideas was challenged over 25 years ago in research conducted by Bouchard *et al.* (1974). In one experiment participants working alone and in small groups were asked to think about novel and unlikely situations (for example, 'What would happen if everybody went blind?' or 'What if everybody had two thumbs on each hand?'). The number of ideas generated by individuals working alone and in groups of four to seven were compared. As Figure 3.5 shows, individuals generated more ideas than groups of four or seven people; that is, groups working together perform *worse* than the same number of individuals working alone. This finding has been repeatedly reported in empirical research (Paulus *et al.*, 1993; Stroebe *et al.*, 1992).

Earlier research by Taylor *et al.* (1958) asks individuals working alone and four-person groups to attempt to solve problems

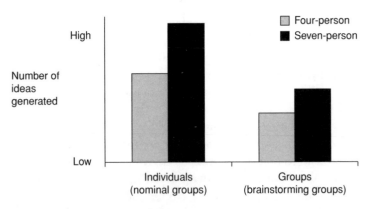

FIGURE 3.5 Ideas generated by nominal and brainstorming groups. Note that individuals working alone produced more ideas than brainstorming groups regardless of group size

Source: adapted from Bouchard et al. (1974)

using brainstorming. Results showed that the four-person interacting groups produced almost twice as many ideas than the average number produced by individuals working alone. However, it has to be remembered that the amount of person-time spent by the four-person group was really four times that of the individual working alone. To take this into account the researchers combined the ideas of four individuals (this was done by randomly putting four individuals into what were called 'nominal groups'). When these nominal groups were compared to the interacting groups, the researchers found that the nominal groups produced nearly twice as many ideas in a set time compared to the interacting groups. Not only did these nominal groups produce a greater quantity of ideas, but subsequent analysis of the ideas also showed the nominal groups to produce better quality ideas. More recent research has also confirmed these findings (Mullen *et al.*, 1991). From this it seems that brainstorming may be most effective in nominal groups, or where individuals are working on their own and not interacting with other people.

The research we have considered above questions the effectiveness of brainstorming as an effective technique for problem-solving in small, interacting groups. Three main explanations have been put forward to account for this lack of effectiveness; these are production blocking, evaluation apprehension and social loafing.

Production blocking occurs where the ideas of an individual are blocked or unable to be expressed to the rest of the group because they are waiting for an opportunity to speak and forgetting ideas while waiting. In addition, a person might get distracted by the ideas of another and hence start thinking more about the suggested idea, with the consequence that they forget their own idea. Production blocking is not solely to do with opportunity to speak but also because individuals do run out of ideas fairly quickly (Stroebe and Diehl, 1994). The main problem, and cause of production blocking, is the effect on people having to wait to speak or wait their turn in a group setting. Diehl and Stroebe (1991) investigated production blocking in an experiment in which four participants were placed in separate rooms, connected by microphone and asked to conduct a brainstorming session for 15 minutes on ways in which disabled people could be better integrated into society. In one condition, participants were allowed to speak or contribute whenever they wanted to; in another condition, participants had to wait their turn in a predetermined sequence; in the third condition, participants had to press a button when they had something to offer so that they could go on a 'waiting list'. Comparison of ideas from each of these conditions was made with four participants working alone on the topic and having the results combined afterwards (nominal groups – see section 3.5.4). In all brainstorming conditions the nominal group performed the best. The 'waiting list' condition resulted in the poorest group productivity. The other two conditions fell in between with regard to group productivity.

Evaluation apprehension reflects the concerns an individual has – as we saw with social facilitation – of being evaluated by other people. In the context of brainstorming, the instruction to voice any idea they have may cause anxiety when the person suspects that the idea is outrageous, highly unusual or silly. Diehl and Stroebe (1987) found support for this explanation from research where participants who worked alone but were led to believe they were being watched and evaluated produce fewer ideas than participants who did not know they were being observed.

Social loafing also offers an explanation of the poorer performance of brainstorming groups to individuals or nominal groups. We considered social loafing in detail in section 3.4 and will not spend time on it here. The main point is that individuals may misperceive how productive each is being and believe that performance is better than it actually is, with the result that people may think they have made enough effort and stop producing ideas (Paulus and Dzindolet, 1993).

Given that consistent evidence over 25 years reports that brainstorming is not an effective technique, it does seem paradoxical that it is still highly regarded and commonly used. This has been explained by Diehl and Stroebe (1991) as the result of the *illusion of group effectiveness*. This is where individuals in a group think that the group is much more effective or performing better than it actually is. After all, the group is usually better than any one average individual. In addition, people may draw on their experience from problem-solving groups, where sharing a right answer may indeed result in a group outperforming the sum of its individuals. The illusion is perpetuated because groups often do not take time properly and objectively to monitor and evaluate their performance. Further, as indicated earlier, individuals enjoy a brainstorming group and may think it is more effective to increase the likelihood of being involved in brainstorming groups in the future. Finally, individuals are not aware of just how much might have been achieved had each member of the group worked alone and subsequently pooled all their ideas.

Electronic brainstorming

The increasing use of e-mail and the internet allows *electronic brainstorming* to take place between people who communicate with each other from different parts of the world and in the absence of face-to-face interaction. In electronic brainstorming each member of the group can input his or her own ideas without waiting to speak or take turns and then send these ideas to the others in the group. The screen then displays all the other group members' ideas as well as the individual operating the computer. Gallupe *et al.* (1991) compared the performance of traditional brainstorming groups with that of electronic brainstorming groups and found that the performance of the latter greatly exceeded that of the former. Electronic brainstorming groups are probably more similar to nominal groups than interacting groups, hence we might expect better performance. However, there does seem to be a limiting factor in group size. Dennis and Valacich (1993) reported that electronic brainstorming increased creativity compared to nominal groups for 12-person groups but not 6-person groups. Globalisation, together with the rapidly increasing use of electronic means of communication, may result in the illusion of effectiveness of brainstorming becoming a reality.

Other techniques

Two other techniques are worthy of mention, although they are less widely known or used; these are the nominal group technique and the Delphi technique.

The *nominal group technique* (Delbecq *et al.*, 1975) involves a three-stage process in which individuals in a group work alone, perhaps in the same room, but without communicating with each other. During this stage each individual writes down his or her ideas or possible solutions to the problem at hand. The second stage involves each member of the group communicating his or her ideas to the others in the group. No discussion or comment about the ideas takes place at this stage. The third and final stage is where ideas or solutions are discussed and evaluated, and group agreement achieved on which to adopt or implement as appropriate. The main advantages of this technique are that competition and domination of one or two individuals in the idea-generation stage is eliminated. Group participation then follows and commitment to outcomes or decisions reached is achieved.

The *Delphi technique* avoids face-to-face interaction and involves ideas or solutions being made by individuals, but anonymously. One person collects together all ideas generated and then circulates these to the other group members for comment and evaluation. This is repeated until a group consensus or majority opinion is achieved that is acceptable to the whole group. The Delphi technique has the main drawback of being time-consuming, and may feel artificial to those involved since no 'real' communication takes place. However, it has been shown to be more effective than brainstorming (Jewell and Reitz, 1981).

Individual and group performance

This chapter started by raising the issue of how individuals behave and perform in relation to small groups. Having considered social facilitation, social loafing and brainstorming in some detail, we are now in a position to offer some comments. First, it is not at all clear that groups, whether one is merely in the presence of, or in interaction with, others, enhance individual performance or are better than individuals. Performing in front of a group or audience enhances performance on well-learned or easy tasks but impairs performance on complex or novel tasks. Co-acting groups, such as those typically investigated for evidence of social loafing, often perform less well than maximum individual effort might lead us to expect. Furthermore, the commonly accepted wisdom of brainstorming as an effective technique is seriously questioned by consistent empirical evidence. Groups therefore do not often, or perhaps usually, perform as well as the same number of individuals working alone.

Second, in view of what has just been said, there is the question of why, in business, industry and other aspects of human endeavour, we have such faith and commitment to working in groups. The illusion of group effectiveness, referred to earlier in this chapter (section 3.5.2), may be applied more generally and reflect the social need that belonging to and working in groups serves for individuals. Finally, it is important to remember that we have not considered a wide enough range of individual and group performances to accept the generalisations made in the previous two points. Further and different types of considerations are given in Chapter 7 when we look at individual and group decision-making.

Summary

This chapter has looked at theory and empirical research concerning how individuals perform both in the presence of others and in interaction. Research has shown that people prefer to work with others, especially on complex tasks, new tasks and in threatening situations. Social facilitation takes place where individual performance is enhanced by the presence of other people. Social facilitation occurs when a task is easy or well learned; by contrast, impairment of performance in the presence of others occurs with a complex or new task. Social facilitation has been explained through Zajonc's drive theory. This relies on the arousal effect of an audience which is explained by evaluation apprehension and distraction–conflict. Social loafing is said to have occurred where individual effort or performance decreases in a group setting and is also a function of group size. Social loafing has been explained using social impact theory and the collective effort model. Brainstorming is a technique designed to facilitate a group to produce more ideas or generally perform better. Research over twenty-five years has consistently shown individuals to perform better (per person) than a brainstorming group. The relatively poorer performance of brainstorming groups may be due to production blocking, evaluation apprehension and social loafing. People hold an illusion of group effectiveness which reflects a belief that groups perform better, in a wide range of tasks and situations, than individuals. Research does not strongly support this.

Further reading

Levine, J. M. and Moreland, R. L. (1998) Small groups. In D. T. Gilbert, S. T. Fiske and G. Lindzey (eds), *The Handbook of Social Psychology* (4th edn), New York: McGraw-Hill. Provides a wider coverage of topics than this chapter, but is up-to-date and a central source of detailed theory and empirical research. Useful for other chapters in this text also.

Baron, R. S., Kerr, N. and Miller, N. (1992) *Group Processes, Group Decision, Group Action*, Milton Keynes: Open University Press. Broad coverage of all major areas of group processes; provides more detail, in respect of the theory and research, for the topics discussed in this chapter. Good, but looking a little dated now.

Napier, R. W. and Gershenfeld, M. K. (1999) *Groups: Theory and Experience* (6th edn), Boston, MA: Houghton Mifflin Company. Another broad text, but has more applied emphasis and is packed with lots of exercises and practical tasks that you can carry out yourself to demonstrate the areas covered in this chapter.

Chapter 4

Group development and group structure

Introduction

I MAGINE THAT YOU HAVE just started a new job and will be working with a team of six other people preparing high-quality sandwiches and lunches for a famous chain of stores. On your first day all will seem new and strange to you, and you will need to quickly find out who is the leader of the team, what your role is, and how members of the group work together to perform their tasks effectively and efficiently.

Now imagine a different situation where you, along with ten other people, have just formed a self-help group to support each other in learning and understanding statistics on the course in psychology that you are taking. The group is new, and while some of you know others in the group to some degree, there are people whom you have not met before. One of the first tasks the group will have to decide is how it will work, what the rules will be and what are the different problems with statistics each of you is experiencing.

These two different examples of small groups highlight key questions that you are likely to ask, and represent the areas of group development and group structure well. In this chapter we will look at theory and research concerning how groups develop and how a new member of a group becomes socialised into the rules, norms and roles in the group. We will also look at the effect of group size on performance and then consider the important area of group structure. In looking at group structure we will cover the areas of cohesiveness, norms, status and roles (and role strain and role conflict) and communication structure. We start with a newly formed group and consider how it develops to become established and effective.

Group development

Imagine that you have been selected to work on a new project, either at work or with other students for an assignment, and have been allocated to work with a small group of people whom you have not met or worked with before. This is a common situation facing many project teams in industry or a business organisation. The prime objective of the group is to work effectively together at the allocated task. This raises the interesting question of how a group develops and changes over a period of time. Social psychologists have suggested that a group goes through five stages of development (Tuckman, 1965; see also Moreland and Levine, 1982). These stages are called forming, storming, norming, performing and adjourning. Some groups may go through all five of these stages while others may not progress beyond a certain stage or will return at times to repeat certain stages.

Forming is the initial stage of development for a group and one in which members get acquainted with each other, discovering each other's backgrounds, attitudes and experiences. Two key factors may be dependent on the group leader, if one has been appointed. The first is to provide structure and establish ground rules. The second feature is the orientation of the group to the task set and agreement about the objectives. The forming stage is successfully completed if these are achieved and the group has established for itself an identity among its members.

Storming is the second stage and one in which conflict may develop in the group due to potential disagreements between different individual goals and the objectives of the group. There may be disagreement over the priorities that need to be set to achieve the task and the order in which the priorities should be addressed. It is a stage at which bargaining may take place between group members to achieve agreed priorities and ways forward. Group members, especially the leader if there is one, have to manage and resolve conflict and agree how they will organise themselves successfully to complete the task given to the group. Groups that are not able to do this may disband at this stage or go on to become ineffective at the task.

Norming is where the group comes together and a degree of cohesiveness (see section 4.5.1) has developed together with a positive sense of group identity. Group members will be satisfied with the group, and accept and agree rules by which the group will operate. In short, the group will have 'gelled' and overcome conflicts that were apparent in the previous stage. There may be dangers of the group 'gelling' too well or becoming much too cohesive since members may not focus on the task (see Chapter 7, section 7.5, Groupthink, for more on this).

The *performing* stage is where the group gets down to the task set and takes the previously agreed upon priorities in order. Groups that are well managed and have clear ideas of how to achieve the task at this stage will have successfully passed through the storming and norming stages. In this stage group members may work alone, in subgroups or with the group as a whole. Mutual interdependence between group members is a key feature of this stage, resulting in co-operation and commitment.

The final stage, *adjourning*, is most likely to occur in specially put together project teams that have been given a set task which, once achieved, results in the group disbanding. Adjourning may also occur because one or more members have left the group and it is unable to continue with the task. A group which has worked well together and become highly cohesive will be difficult for individuals in the group to leave. A formal group which has completed its task may continue informally because of the rewards individual members get from being together.

Figure 4.1 summarises these five stages and indicates the key features likely to be present at each stage. Research has provided considerable support for this five-stage model of group development (Eisenstat, 1990). The stage to which a group has developed can be assessed through a questionnaire which focuses on two broad areas: the task in hand and evaluation of the group by the individual members. Task areas include: how well individuals understand the goals of the group; how well the group is organised to achieve the goals; and how well problem-solving takes place. Group evaluation areas include: how much conflict is present; the degree of interdependence between the group members; and

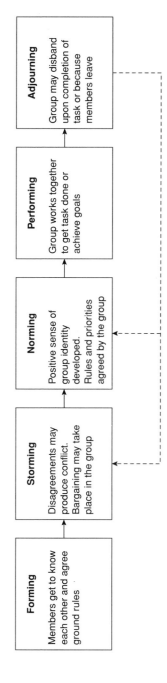

FIGURE 4.1 Five stages of group development. Notice the dotted lines indicate that if the group adjourns because members leave, the group may need to return to a storming or norming stage

how much individuals enjoy being part of the group (Buchan and Huczynski, 1997).

Becoming a member of a group

The five-stage model of group development considered above can be applied both to groups that have a fixed life-span and will disband when the task has been achieved and to groups that are much more enduring. In both cases, but particularly the latter, individuals leave and new members join the group. How individuals new to an established group are socialised to become an effective group member will be considered next.

Group socialisation

A model of *group socialisation* has been proposed by Moreland and Levine (1984, 1989) in which the newcomer to the group makes a judgement about the value of belonging to the group, decides the level of commitment he or she is going to make to the group and its goals, and goes through role transition when moving from being a newcomer to an accepted and experienced member of the group. Moreland and Levine suggest that there are five stages of group socialisation, which reflect mutual evaluation and influence between the newcomer and the established group members. These five stages are summarised in Figure 4.2.

In the *investigation* stage the group may go through formal recruitment and selection processes to find a new group member or one may be allocated by management in an organisation. Whichever method of investigation is used the newcomer enters the group as a new member. *Socialisation* refers to the stage where the group helps the newcomer to understand the goals, rules, norms and so on that operate in the group. At the same time the existing group must adapt to the newcomer and may have to make adjustments to existing modes of operation to do this. Having to make too much adjustment may occur when there

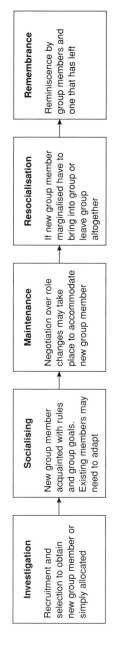

FIGURE 4.2 Five-stage model of socialisation which takes place when a new member joins the group

Source: after Moreland & Levine (1984)

are a number of newcomers to a group. This may take the group back to the storming stage we considered in the previous section.

The *maintenance* stage is where roles of individuals are considered and often changed as a result of the new member. This may happen because the newcomer may bring more experience or skills than already exist in the group, resulting in changes in roles of other members.

The fourth stage is *resocialisation*, which may occur where the group may not have successfully redistributed and changed roles to accommodate the newcomer. If these matters cannot be resolved the newcomer may become marginalised in the group. If resocialisation from being marginalised cannot be achieved, the newcomer is likely to leave the group. Resocialisation may also be achieved by an existing group member leaving the group to allow the newcomer to become an integral part.

The final stage is *remembrance* which takes place when the remaining group members and the individual who has left the group reminisce and reflect on their time and experience with the group. Memories may be good or bad; either way individuals also try to learn from the experience.

Initial entry into the group and leaving a group is often marked by rituals, rites of passage or initiation rites, which may be enjoyable, humiliating or quite painful.

Initiation rites

You have just started a new job working in a manufacturing company with a small team responsible for orders for spare parts. It is your first day and one of the team says to you, 'Go down to the stores and ask John for a long wait'. So off you trot, eager and naively helpful and you ask John for a long wait. He says 'OK, just stand over there and I'll sort you out'. Two hours later you are still there. So you go back to John to ask what the problem is, and he says, 'No problem, you did ask for a long wait, and that is what you have had!' You go back to your team and they all have a good laugh at your expense.

Initiation rites or rites of passage, such as the above example, are common when somebody is a new member of a group. The example above is mildly embarrassing for the person, and in part the rest of the group is testing to see what you are like. However, entry to some groups can involve quite extreme initiation rites and sometimes go too far. Initiation rites serve numerous functions, one of which is to make the new member feel committed to the group he or she is joining.

A classic experiment conducted by Aronson and Mills (1959) highlights a number of important points in this respect. In this study, female students volunteered to join a discussion group on the topic of the psychology of sex. They were told that before they could join they would have to be screened to see if they were able to discuss sex openly with other people. This was the initiation stage of the experiment. One-third of the female students were put in a 'severe initiation' condition in which they had to recite aloud a list of swear-words. Another third were put in the 'mild initiation' condition in which they had to recite words related to sex but not obscene words. Finally, the remaining third were allowed to join the discussion group without any prior initiation condition. The female participants then listened to a group discussion, using headphones, which was on the topic of the psychology of sex but designed to be dull and extremely boring. The researchers then asked each participant after she had listened to the boring discussion how interesting she found it and how much she enjoyed listening to the conversation.

As can be seen from Figure 4.3, results confirmed the predictions of the experimenters in that female students who had gone through a severe initiation found the discussion enjoyable and the participants in the discussion interesting. By contrast, those in the mild initiation and control conditions were less interested either in the discussion or those participating in the discussion.

Notwithstanding possible alternative explanations (such as the possibility that the recitations in the 'severe' initiation created a genuine interest in the 'boring' discussion), this research clearly demonstrates that if someone invests a lot of effort to gain entry to a group then that person is likely to see the group as interesting

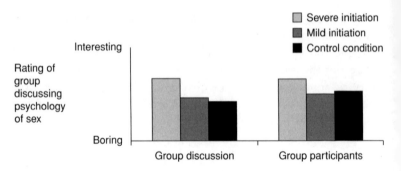

FIGURE 4.3 Ratings of group discussion and participants in the gro
following mild, severe, or no initiation

Source: adapted from Aronson and Mills (1959)

and worthwhile, even if in reality it is not. This is an example of *cognitive dissonance* (Festinger, 1957), a theory of central importance in social psychology. In the context of initiation rites and the above experiment, cognitive dissonance theory states that when two cognitions are inconsistent, an unpleasant psychological state of tension is created. In this context, the two cognitions are: 'I have made a lot of effort to join this group' and 'this group is boring'. Since you cannot change the former cognition the latter is changed and you believe the group to be interesting. For more on cognitive dissonance see Pennington *et al.* (1999).

The general point to take from this research is that rites of initiation serve to create commitment and value for the new member joining a group. Once a person has been with the group for some time they may come to see how it really is; in a sense, the 'honeymoon' period will be over.

Group size

Group size is a topic that is often neglected in books on group behaviour, where it is often included under the heading of social loafing. We saw in Chapter 3 that as group size increases, average individual effort tends to decrease. As we saw, this can be countered by making the task of value to the individuals in the group or clearly relating outcomes to rewards for the individual. In what follows we shall look at group size from two perspectives: in small groups in relation to communication and group performance, and, by contrast, in large groups where individual identity becomes submerged.

Small groups

The size of a group has been shown to affect overall behaviour and individual aspects in a number of ways. Research shows that smaller groups, of between three and eight, are faster at completing tasks than are larger groups of 12 or more members (Shaw, 1981). However, this is not always the case and may depend on the nature of the task facing the group. For example, a diverse task such as information-gathering and fact-finding is carried out more effectively by a larger group. This is because the task can be broken down into different components and specific subtasks allocated to different members of the group. By contrast, smaller groups are more effective at using information to come to a decision. Hence, groups of between five and seven are often seen as ideal for decision-making and taking action.

Size is also an important factor in terms of relationships and communication between individual members. Kephart (1950) produced a surprising set of statistics showing how the number of relations, one-to-one and subgroups, rises dramatically as the number in the group increases. For example, with two people there is obviously only one relationship, with three people the number of relationships rises to six (three within pairs, and three two-to-one combinations), and with four people the number of relationships rises to 25. By the time you have seven people in a group the number of possible relationships becomes nearly a thousand (966 to be precise). No wonder communication, conflict and consensual agreement are issues with larger groups. Larger groups, of say seven or more, do have a tendency to break down into smaller subgroups. Gebhardt and Meyers (1995) demonstrated that subgroups have a greater likelihood of influencing the decision of a group, especially when members of a subgroup regularly communicate with each other throughout the period of decision-making.

The behaviour of individuals may be different in smaller and larger groups. Mullen *et al.* (1989) found that individuals in small groups are much more self-conscious and sensitive to behaviour appropriate and inappropriate to the small group setting. By contrast in larger groups, individual self-awareness is reduced and there is less concern about self-regulation of behaviour. This may be because in a larger group a person feels more anonymous and his or her contribution to the outcome less obvious (akin to explanations of social loafing in some ways). It may also be more difficult for the individual to be noticed and heard in a larger group and inappropriate behaviour may be a way, albeit dysfunctional, to remedy this.

Opportunity to contribute to group discussion declines with larger groups and it is easier for some individuals to dominate discussion than in a smaller group. Because of this, larger groups tend to find it more difficult to reach a decision or the solution to a problem than smaller groups (Shaw, 1981). Individual morale is also affected by group size: as a group's size increases, morale declines; this pattern is also in evidence in relation to the liking of one group member for others in the group (Kerr and Braun, 1981).

The number of individuals likely to dominate a group changes with size. For example, in a 20-person group five people or fewer tend to dominate; and in a 10-person group it is often just three people who dominate. In smaller groups of five or six or fewer, it is easy for one or two individuals to dominate, and contributions of each group member tend to be more equal (Napier and Gershenfeld, 1999).

Deindividuation

It was indicated above that with larger groups individuals become less concerned about self-regulation of behaviour. *Deindividuation* is characterised as an individual's feelings of loss of personal identity, increased feeling of anonymity and consequential decrease in personal responsibility for action (Zimbardo, 1970). Social psychologists have associated deindividuation with crowd settings (very, very, large groups) or smaller groups, but where some means of decreasing personal identity to make everyone look alike or be indistinguishable in a small group is achieved. As such, deindividuation has been associated with loss of control and restraint and has been invoked to explain riots, mob behaviour, lynchings in the United States of America, and other antisocial behaviour (Zimbardo, 1970). Mullen (1986) claims that the larger the group or mob, the more individuals lose self-awareness and become willing to commit atrocities.

Zimbardo (1970) conducted a classic study to demonstrate the effect of individual anonymity in a small group. In this experiment college students were each dressed in identical clothes and wore a hood over their heads that concealed their faces but allowed them to see each other. Individuals who were 'deindividuated' in this way were not allowed to call each other by their names. By contrast, in another condition, individual identity was enhanced by ensuring that each individual in the group knew each other's names and they wore clothes of their own choosing. Individuals were then asked to deliver electric shocks to others who were really confederates of the experimenter. In fact no electric shocks were delivered but the participants were not aware of this at the time. Zimbardo found, as predicted, that higher levels of electric shocks were delivered by participants in deindividuated than in the individuated small groups. This was particularly the case when deindividuated participants had previously met the person to whom they were to deliver shocks and that person had been rude to them.

The assumption that this and subsequent supporting research on deindividuation makes is that anonymity acts to let loose antisocial and destructive behaviour on the part of the individual. However, an alternative and convincing model has been put forward by Reicher (1987) which basically states that being part of a crowd or increasing anonymity in a small group acts to enhance the individual's identification with the group. This, in turn, results in individuals being made much more aware of group norms.

Earlier research by Johnson and Downing (1979) can be seen to support Reicher's model. In this experiment participants were asked to dress in anonymous clothes and wear a hood, similar to Zimbardo's experiment, or dress in a nurse's uniform. The latter are associated with norms of helping and caring, the former with more sinister groups such as the Klu Klux Klan in America. Participants in both conditions were asked to deliver electric shocks to somebody when they had got an answer wrong. As can be seen from Figure 4.4, deindividuation through hooded clothes or a nurse's uniform resulted in higher levels of shock in the former case and lower in the latter. Those dressed in a nurse's uniform chose to decrease levels of shock, while hooded participants increased levels of shock.

In summary, initial theory and research on deindividuation suggested that anonymity or sameness enhanced people's antisocial behaviour. Other work suggests that deindividuation makes group norms more salient or accessible in a person's mind, with

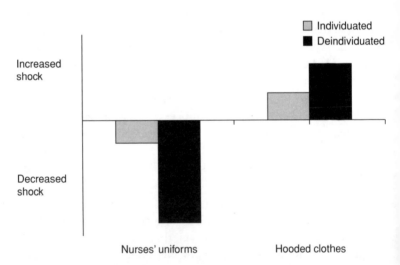

FIGURE 4.4 Deindividuation enhances group norms with participants dressed in a nurse's uniform decreasing levels of shock whilst those in hooded clothes increased levels of shock

Source: adapted from Johnson and Downing (1979)

the consequence that people act in accordance with the prevailing norms of the group. Deindividuation therefore highlights the importance of group norms, and we will consider this and other aspects of group structure in section 4.5.

Group structure

Group structure refers to 'the inter-relationships between the individuals constituting the group, and the guidelines to group behaviour that make group functioning orderly and predictable' (Greenberg and Baron, 1993, p.278). In what follows we will consider four aspects of group structure: cohesiveness, norm, status and roles. We shall extend the consideration of roles to include role ambiguity and role strain.

Cohesiveness

Group cohesiveness may be regarded as the 'glue' that holds a small group of people together. Cohesiveness refers to the extent to which members of the group are attracted to each other, accept and agree with the priorities and goals of the group and contribute to help achieving the goals.

A certain level of cohesiveness must exist for any small group to be able to work together, and groups that lack cohesiveness may be characterised by members who dislike each other and are unable to agree on the group's tasks and objectives. At the extreme, a lack of cohesiveness will result in a group disbanding or being so dysfunctional that it fails to achieve tasks that have been set. A certain level of cohesiveness is a basic requirement for any group to be able to function, and is recognised by organisations and senior managers in companies as being desirable (Buchan and Huczynski, 1997). Given this, it is clearly important to understand what factors contribute to making a group cohesive.

We have already seen, in section 4.3.2, that severity of initiation of new members into the group increases both liking for the group as a whole and individuals in the group (Aronson and Mills,

1959). Other factors which have been identified include: attractiveness of the group; the opportunity to interact with members of the group; shared common goals; stable group membership; small size; past experience of success of the group; external threat, and status congruence (Buchanan and Huczynski, 1997).

Where the group is operating in an environment of high external threat or severe competition with another group, cohesiveness tends to increase. Faced with a 'common enemy' members of a group tend to pull together and put aside minor, internal differences. This was most dramatically demonstrated in Sherif's famous and classic summer camp experiment with 11- to 12-year-old schoolboys (Sherif *et al.*, 1961). Here two groups, the Rattlers and the Eagles, competed with each other for prizes or privileges. As competition increased each group became more cohesive. *Status congruence*, which is equal status between groups, enhances cohesiveness since agreement among the group members of the status hierarchy (see section 4.5.3) within the group means that the individuals in the group are happy to work with the established status structure.

Highly cohesive groups are generally effective in achieving goals and solving problems while at the same time providing a positive experience for individual group members. Highly cohesive groups are participative on the part of members, accept group goals, and evidence low absenteeism (Cartwright, 1968). However, there are downsides, and these occur because the group members enjoy being part of the group and in the presence of other members so much that they may lose sight of the goals of the group or work counter to the interests of the organisation. We will explore one aspect of this more fully in Chapter 7 when we consider the phenomenon of *groupthink*. Figure 4.5 summarises the contributory factors and consequences of group cohesiveness.

Hogg (1992) offers a wider perspective by suggesting that group cohesiveness is representative of the more general phenomenon of social cohesion which can be related to how larger groups such as cultures or nations are held together.

Finally, cohesive groups may be characterised as displaying *synergy* (Hall, 1971). Synergy means that a group is seen to be

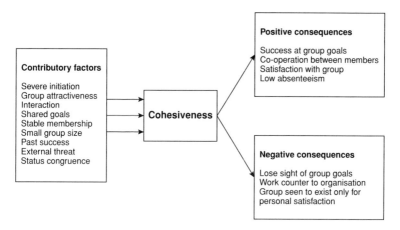

FIGURE 4.5 Contributory factors to and consequences of high group cohesiveness

more than the sum of its individual members, with synergistic groups performing better than the most able or best individual in the group.

Group norms

Group norms are the rules by which a group operates. Norms are both prescriptive in the sense that they provide guidelines on how individuals should behave, and proscriptive in stating behaviours which should be avoided. Group norms are usually informal and not written down, as opposed to formal rules such as written statements about the scope and purpose of a committee in an organisation. Adherence to group norms is usually a requirement of continued membership of the group.

Pressures to conform to group norms are often intense, and while norms may allow for a range of behaviour there will be limits as to what a group will tolerate. Group norms can influence performance at work, attitudes and values, and decision-making. The pressure to conform here results from *normative* social influence rather than *informational* social influence.

An experiment by Mitchell *et al.* (1985) demonstrated how the work norms of other people influenced individual performance.

Here college students were given the task of placing ice-cream lids on the container. Two experimental conditions were used. In one condition, students completed the task facing a wall with charts showing production levels of other workers. In the second condition, the same production levels were provided but this time through working with other people on the same task. Mitchell *et al.* (1985) found that students matched the production level of others when working with them much more than when exposed to charts on the wall. It may be concluded from these findings that working with others produces social pressure to conform to the production norms of the group.

Solomon Asch's (1951, 1955) famous experiments on conformity demonstrated how the judgements of others in a group, even if apparently incorrect, cause others to conform to the majority view. Asch found that a unanimous view produces the greatest pressure on an individual to conform; if there is one other person who disagrees with the majority view, conformity levels of the individual under study drop quite dramatically (see Chapter 5).

How groups develop group norms, especially in newly established groups, has been extensively researched. In existing groups we have already seen how a new member is socialised into a group and adopts the prevailing norms of the group (see section 4.3.1). Feldman (1984) has suggested four main factors that contribute to the development and establishment of norms; these are from: precedents set over time; carry-overs from other situations; explicit statements made by others, and critical events in the history of the group. These factors are shown in Figure 4.6 together with an example of each.

Group norms, once established, are very hard to change, and change will only come about if the group experiences *disequilibrium* (Lewin, 1947). Disequilibrium occurs when a group is in crisis or members are highly dissatisfied with the group. When one or both of these are present (they often go together), changes in how the group operates will have to be made for the group to continue and function more effectively. Change may occur from within through minority influence (Mugny and Pérez, 1991) which often comes from a high-status person in the group. Change may

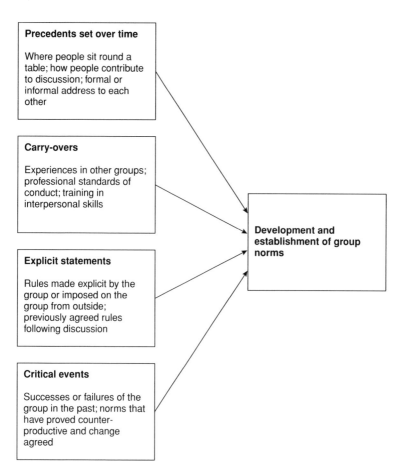

FIGURE 4.6 Four key factors involved in the development of group norms

Source: after Feldman (1984)

also come from outside the group (e.g., organisational changes, company mergers, changes in government policy).

Group norms, then, are the unwritten, largely social rules by which a group operates. Individuals are required to conform to existing norms and may be excluded from the group if they do not. Norms exert powerful pressures towards conformity and are hard to change.

Group status

Status refers to an individual's standing or position of prestige in a group; status may be formal or informal. Formal status may be defined as 'a collection of rights and obligations associated with a position' (Buchan and Huczynski, 1997). This means that position exists regardless of who occupies it, for example, the chief executive of a company, middle and senior managers, or the leader in a group. It is interesting to note that formal status hierarchies, of which we may be unaware, often exist in groups; only by being a member of the group does the status hierarchy become revealed. Figure 4.7 demonstrates this in relation to a local group or 'chapter' of Hell's Angels motorcyclists.

Formal status usually has status symbols attached to the position, with the status symbol being more prestigious or indicative of a person's position in a group or organisation (e.g. plush office or large desk for senior manager, and smaller desk and shared office, but perhaps with own telephone, for junior manager).

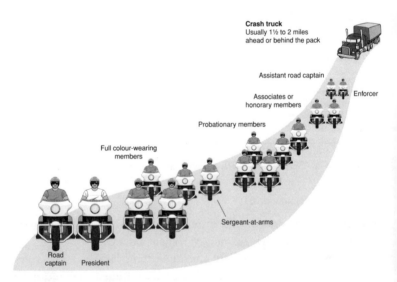

FIGURE 4.7 Status hierarchy and position of occupants in a Hell's Angels group when 'on the road'

Source: after Sewer (1992)

Informal status may come about through, for example, length of time in the job, older and more experienced team or group members, or individuals who have special skills or qualifications not formally recognised but seen as being of value to the group. In the latter example this may be, say, having a professor in a group. This may enhance the standing and general prestige of the group to outsiders and group members alike. Informal status may also be negative when stereotypes or prejudice cause a person who may occupy a higher status position in the group to be viewed in other respects as low status. This may result in status incongruence (Secord and Backman, 1974) between formal and informal statuses. This is not desirable and the individual will seek to achieve status congruence – the same level of status or position in the group on a number of different dimensions.

The characterisation of formal and informal status that we have considered relates to Van Dijt and Wilke's (1993) concepts of specific status characteristics and diffuse status characteristics. Here formal status is associated with the former and informal with the latter. Diffuse status characteristics held by an individual may result in generalisation across a range of different tasks since generally favourable expectations are held of that person. High diffuse status will enhance the specific status of an individual resulting in the person having high prestige and influence in the group.

Two important features are associated with people who occupy high-status positions. First, a tendency to initiate ideas and activities that the rest of the group takes up and responds to. Second, what is called *consensual privilege*, which is the positive evaluation and recognition of the high status of the position by other members of the group. Clearly, these represent some of the characteristics of group leaders – a topic we will explore in some detail in Chapter 6.

Group roles

Roles in a group may be defined as 'the sets of behaviours that individuals occupying specific positions in a group are expected to perform' (Baron and Byrne, 2001, p. 483). As such, roles, like status positions, both describe and prescribe the behaviour of a person occupying a role. Roles are a common and pervasive feature of both formal and informal groups extending across work groups, family groups, teenage gangs, Hell's Angels groups and so on. *Role differentiation* refers to how different people perform different roles within a group. Role differentiation may emerge as a natural process or be a consequence of allocation to a formal role (e.g. group leader, finance officer, note-taker). Roles will often have norms of behaviour associated with them, but are interpreted differently depending on the individual's personality, for example, and interpretation of the role.

Roles serve three main functions. First, they allow for a division of labour to take place among the members of a group; this should result in efficient operation of the group on the task set. Second, roles bring order and predictability to the group; individuals know their own role and the roles of other people in the group. Third, a role provides a sense of identity for a person; roles may be associated with status and give the person standing among others, and enhance that person's self-esteem.

Many different types of roles exist in groups – we explore leadership roles and different team roles in Chapters 6 and 7 respectively. Slater (1955), using a system of recording group interaction developed by Bales (1950) – see Chapter 2 – noticed that groups were often characterised by two different leadership roles. One leadership role is the task leader whose main concern is to ensure that the group gets on with the task in hand. Another leadership role is called the socio-emotional leader who is more concerned to ensure that good relationships exist between members of the group and that conflict is resolved should it arise. Both types of leadership role are important for a group to work effectively, but this depends on the situation or environment in which the group is operating (see Chapter 6, section 6.5.1 on Fielder's contingency theory of leadership). Another role relates much more to the style and personality of the individual, and has been called 'the self-oriented role' (Benne and Sheats, 1948). This includes 'blockers' – where the person is stubborn and resistant in the group; 'recognition seekers' – where the person is always trying to gain the attention of others in the group; and 'dominators' and 'avoiders' – people who keep their distance and do not fully engage with the group.

An individual may occupy a number of different roles in different groups or multiple roles within one group. Sometimes this leads to role strain or role conflict.

Role strain and role conflict

Role strain refers to the difficulties a person experiences when performing or trying to enact a particular role. This may be caused by the person lacking the skills, experience or expertise needed to perform the role effectively or by external forces. Externally, for example, other group members may have unrealistic expectations of the role or may regard how the role is enacted to be different from how the individual occupying the role is actually performing that role (Secord and Backman, 1974). Disagreement over the way in which a role should be performed may result from one or more of the following four factors:

1 Different group members may disagree on what should be expected from the role.
2 There may be disagreement over the range of behaviours associated with a role and what is prohibited.
3 Members may disagree about appropriate situations for the role.
4 Members may disagree on what is core and required from the role and what is optional or peripheral.

You may wish to analyse a particular role (e.g. student, husband or wife, father or mother) from each of these four sources of disagreement and see what, if anything, may cause role strain for you.

Role strain may be resolved by the individual in one of three ways. First, by conforming to the expectations of others for the role, thus putting aside individual interpretation. Second, by trying to negotiate a compromise between his or her interpretation and other group members' interpretation of the role. Third, by ignoring other people's expectations for the role and enacting it as he or she thinks fit. The latter strategy is likely to lead to group conflict and hence should be avoided (Gross *et al.*, 1958).

Role conflict results from the fact that people occupy multiple roles (e.g. mother, daughter, friend, worker). Perhaps the most common source of role conflict is the simultaneous demands that come from having a full-time job and family roles of wife, mother and so on. Role conflict is also likely to occur between the role of student and role of employee. Williams *et al.* (1991) report that role conflict is not just unpleasant but highly stressful as well. Conflict between roles may be difficult to resolve, but at times of crises a hierarchy of roles often emerges which dictates how a person will behave. For example, Killian (1952) reports a case where disaster struck in a town in Texas which threatened both place of work and home. Most workers prioritised their families and left work. Similar role conflict operates for police officers, firemen, nurses and doctors. In the normal course of life people are able to manage and adjust to the different demands placed on them by occupying many different roles in society.

Putting it all together

In this section we have looked at four main components of group structure which affect both how the group functions and the various types of relationships that exist and develop between the members of a group. If we also include communication structure, which we looked at in Chapter 1, we can see five main components as shown in Figure 4.8. For a group to operate effectively in terms of achieving the task set and to the satisfaction of the individual group members, all these components come together to operate in a complex way and determine the unique structure of a group.

Summary

Group development is typically characterised by forming, storming, norming, performing and adjourning. These stages may be

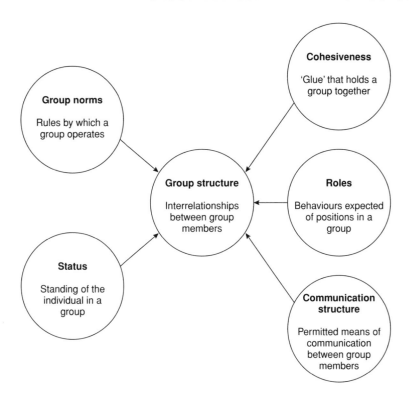

FIGURE 4.8 Five components of group structure which affect performance, stability and effectiveness of a group

returned to by an established group when circumstances change. A new person who joins a group will be socialised into the goals, rules and norms of the group. The roles of group members may change to accommodate the new member of the group. Often new members go through initiation rites before being accepted by the group.

Group size is an important and often neglected variable. Groups of between three and eight are usually faster at completing tasks than larger groups. In small groups, individuals may be more self-conscious. In very large groups, crowds or nations, deindividuation may occur; this is where individuals feel anonymous and are more likely to conform to group norms.

Group structure refers to interrelationships between group members and rules of behaviour that allow a group to function in an orderly way. The five main aspects of group structure are: cohesiveness, norms, status, roles and communication structure. Cohesiveness is the 'glue' that holds a group together, and relates to how attracted each member of the group is to the group itself and other members of the group. Group cohesiveness increases in a threatening environment.

Norms are the rules by which groups operate, and can be both prescriptive and proscriptive. Pressures to conform to group norms may be normative or informational. Status refers to an individual's standing in a group, and may be both formal and informal. High-status people are characterised as initiators of ideas and have consensual privilege. Roles are the set of behaviours that individuals who occupy certain positions in a group are expected to perform (e.g. the leadership role, or expert role). Role strain and role conflict cause problems for an individual in a group.

Further reading

Brown, R. (2000) *Group Processes: Dynamics Within and Between Groups* (2nd edn), Oxford: Blackwell. The second edition of a book that has become well regarded with good, sustained, critical analysis. Has extended sections on group development and group structure.

Napier, R. W. and Gershenfeld, M. K. (1999) *Groups: Theory and Experience* (6th edn), Boston, MA: Houghton Mifflin. An established text used quite widely in organisational psychology. Has useful chapter on group norms which also deals with deviation from norms. Lots of activities that you can work on with peers or in class.

Greenberg, J. and Baron. R. A. (1993) *Behaviour in Organisations* (5th edn), Boston, MA: Allyn and Bacon. A useful text, if a little dated, with plenty of case studies and applications of research, theory and concepts of real-life situations in organisations.

Chapter 5

Co-operation, conflict and social influence within small groups

Introduction

I MAGINE THAT YOU HAVE been working with a small group of colleagues – work colleagues or college friends – on a project. The group has met on a number of occasions and differences of opinion have started to emerge on how best to proceed. Up until now the group has got along well and progress on the project has been satisfactory. You have some strong disagreements with the views of others in the group, but at the same time you have a common view with one or two other group members. The group meets again and the differences of opinion among its members are now preventing progress on the project and, more worryingly, threatening to develop into outright conflict within the group. If something is not done to reduce conflict, influence some group members to change their minds and develop a stronger sense of co-operation, the group may be in danger of being so dysfunctional that it will have to disband. The consequence of this would be failure on the project and individuals taking away a bad experience of group work. This bad experience might affect how they inter-act subsequently in small group settings.

This imaginary scenario may sound a little extreme, but think about any small group of which you have been a member and you will no doubt recognise many elements of the above from your own experience.

This chapter explores social psychological research into co-operation, competition, conflict and social influence *within* small groups. We will consider strategies to encourage co-operation, how conflict arises and can be managed, and how majorities and minorities may influence individuals, and hence the group as a whole. It is important to bear in mind from the start that we are concerned to look at what takes place within groups or *intra-group processes*. In this chapter we are not looking at competition and conflict *between* groups or *intergroup conflict*. There is a vast theoretical and research literature on intergroup processes (see c.g. Pennington *et al.*, 1999) which is outside the scope of this book. The focus of intergroup processes is mostly on prejudice and discrimination.

Co-operation and competition

What are the key factors determining whether or not group members co-operate or compete with each other? Clearly there may be personality factors such as an individual's need to achieve (McClelland, 1965) or dominate others. We label some people as 'control freaks', where individuals appear to have a need to control all that happens around them. This seems more akin to a neurotic disorder since ultimate control can never be achieved. In this section we look at how social psychologists have theorised and researched determinants of satisfying individual needs vs. co-operating to achieve group goals.

The prisoner's dilemma

The prisoner's dilemma is one of the most extensively researched two-person decision-making games. It was introduced over 40 years ago by Luce and Raiffa (1957). It is based on a simple dilemma – whether to trust another person and co-operate, or act in what is believed to be a person's own best interests. To understand this better we will look at the classic prisoner's dilemma.

Two criminals have been arrested by the police for theft. The police only have enough evidence to charge the two men with a minor crime, but know they have committed a more serious offence. The two 'prisoners' are put into separate rooms for questioning. The police offer each prisoner a choice: the detective tells each that he has enough evidence to secure a conviction on the lesser charge, but if the prisoner confesses and implicates the other person, he will go free and the other person will be convicted of the more serious charge. However, if both prisoners confess, each

	Prisoner A does not confess	Prisoner A does confess
Prisoner B does not confess	**1** Prisoner A gets one year Prisoner B gets one year	**2** Prisoner A goes free Prisoner B gets ten years
Prisoner B does confess	**3** Prisoner A gets ten years Prisoner B goes free	**4** Prisoner A gets five years Prisoner B gets five years

FIGURE 5.1 The prisoner's dilemma. Co-operation and the best mutual outcome is represented by Box 1. Competition and worst mutual outcome is represented by Box 4

will receive a moderate sentence. If neither confesses, the minor offence will merit a light sentence.

Each prisoner separately faces the same dilemma. Should he confess or not? The dilemma is summarised in Figure 5.1, and is represented by what is called a 'pay-off matrix'.

If each prisoner looks at the dilemma from his own, selfish, perspective, each would confess in order to go free, but each acting selfishly would mean both would receive a moderate prison sentence. The best outcome for *both* prisoners is not to confess and both to receive a light sentence. However, for both to adopt this decision, suspicion and lack of trust of the other person must be overcome. Clearly this is difficult when they do not have contact with each other and communication is not allowed. The dilemma facing the two prisoners usually works to the benefit of the police, since it is often easy to arouse a person's suspicions and lack of trust in another.

In the prisoner's dilemma, co-operation and mutual trust result in the best outcome. Competition and mutual mistrust and suspicion result in the worst overall outcome for both people.

This basic experimental matrix, using points or money instead of prison sentences, has been used in a large number of studies and the findings replicated again and again – that mutual distrust results in the worst joint outcome for both people (Dawes, 1991).

Note that, in the way the prisoner's dilemma has been presented to you, the two people are what we have called a 'nominal group' (see Chapter 3), where communication and interaction between the group members has not been allowed. You might think that when two people are allowed to communicate and negotiate, each would adopt the rational decision to co-operate and trust each other. However, research tends not to support this (Carnevale and Pruitt, 1992). This may be because the communication that takes place between the two group members is more in the form of mutual threats – 'if you don't agree with my suggestion it will be worse for both of us' – or some such statement. If the group agrees to employ, for example, a neutral mediator, then co-operation and the best mutual outcome in the prisoner's dilemma tends to be achieved (Welton and Pruitt, 1987). Adopting a competitive or distrustful approach, with mutual disadvantageous outcomes, is likely to occur when individuals are personally and emotionally involved, and the outcomes have important consequences for the individual (Thompson, 1993).

You may think that pay-off matrices such as the prisoner's dilemma represented in Figure 5.1 are an artificial and perhaps meaningless way of investigating co-operation and competition within small groups. However, pay-off matrices do reveal individual differences which affect how a group works. For example, some people play the matrix on a consistently competitive basis and others co-operatively (Kelley and Stahelski, 1970), representing how they are in real life. If a person consistently plays competitively this will usually cause the other person to play competitively too. By contrast, if one person consistently plays co-operatively, a competitive person will exploit this and take advantage of what may be regarded as a weakness in the other person.

The prisoner's dilemma does provide insight into how two people behave when having to decide to trust another or treat the other suspiciously. Even when social interaction and communication takes place the co-operative strategy which results in mutual benefit does not inevitably happen. Outside assistance to facilitate negotiation and trust may be beneficial.

Social dilemmas

Social dilemmas are situations where each person may act selfishly to maximise his or her own personal gain, but if all members of the group operate in this way then the outcomes for all are reduced and everyone loses. For example, water companies impose restrictions on hose-pipes for watering the garden. If everybody abides by the restriction and uses water carefully, no problem will arise. However, if one person persistently uses his hose-pipe to water the garden, others may see this and think 'if he's doing it then I might as well'. Very soon a water shortage problem will exist. The same type of logic may be applied to cars' engine sizes and pollution (the larger the engine, the more pollution produced), as well as traffic jams and only one person in a car (Pennington, 2000).

Two types of social dilemmas have been researched; these are *collective traps* and *collective fences* (Messick and Brewer, 1983). Collective traps are situations where selfish behaviour on the part of the individual is detrimental and negative to the group as a whole – the hose-pipe example above is of this type. By contrast, with collective fences high individual cost is avoided by individuals with the consequence of producing an outcome that is negative to the group as a whole. For example, if you are a member of a society or club, the avoidance of paying subscription fees will benefit you individually (more money in your pocket) but may threaten continuation of the club or society due to insufficient funds. Collective traps are therefore where selfish behaviour by many people ultimately deprives everybody of the resource. Collective fences, by contrast, are where each person in a group avoids a cost and so deprives everybody of the resource.

Social dilemmas have been extensively studied employing an experimental paradigm based on the use of a group resource by individuals in the group (Messick *et al.*, 1983). For example, imagine you belong to a small group of six fishermen where each lives by catching fish from a lake and selling these on to local shops and restaurants. The lake has a certain number of fish and each individual can decide how many to take on any one occasion. After all the members of the group have decided how many to take, the number of fish left is replenished by 10 per cent. Members of the group do the fishing task again and the number of fish left afterwards is again replenished by 10 per cent. This is repeated over many trials. If individuals in the group act selfishly and greedily, the lake will soon have no fish in it and the livelihood for each individual would be gone. If all members of the group co-operate and restraint is used in the number of fish taken, the fish in the lake will last for a long time. A worked example of this is shown in Figure 5.2.

Social dilemmas are common in our everyday lives and frequently present themselves in organisation and work settings. Thus it is important to determine factors that will enhance co-operation and reduce selfish, competitive behaviour. The three most important factors that have been identified are reciprocity, personal orientation towards co-operation, and communication.

Reciprocity is where a person returns the kind of treatment he or she has experienced from other people (Pruitt and Carnevale, 1993). The task then becomes how to encourage people to behave co-operatively to others in the first place so that reciprocation will occur. Knowledge about a social dilemma has been shown to increase co-operation, for example, when a small group is allowed to talk about and discuss a social dilemma in advance of making decisions and, as a result, co-operate more (Jorgenson and Papciak, 1981). Giving precise and accurate information about the resources left (such as the number of fish in the lake) also enhances co-operation among group members (Budescu *et al.*, 1990).

People have been classified as having one of three general *personal orientations* or social motivations when facing a social dilemma (De Dreu and McCusker, 1997). These are co-operative, individualistic and competitive. The individualistic orientation is found where the individual attempts to maximise his or her own

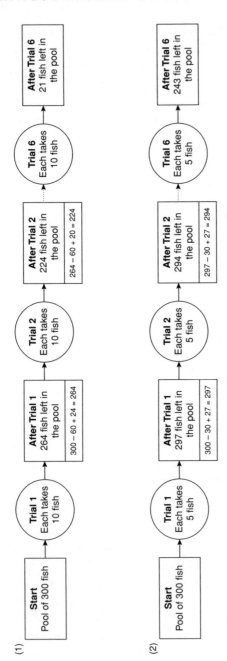

FIGURE 5.2 Example of how selfish behaviour by each individual in a group quickly leads to the lake being depleted of fish (1) and how fish are sustained in the lake by each person co-operating for the common good of the group (2)

Source: adapted from Messick *et al.* (1983)

outcomes; the competitive orientation is where the person is concerned to beat or win against the other person. De Dreu and McCusker (1997) demonstrated that these two orientations, both harmful to the group, could be reduced by couching a task positively rather than negatively.

Communication between group members may enhance co-operation, but as we saw in the previous section with the prisoner's dilemma, this does not follow as a matter of course. Certain conditions are needed for group interaction and communication to result in co-operation. These are that individuals must make a personal commitment to co-operate, and say to other group members that this commitment will be honoured (Kerr *et al.*, 1997).

Conflict in small groups

The small group project scenario given at the start of this chapter painted a fairly bleak picture of a group experiencing a high level of conflict which it was unable to resolve. The potential consequences included failure of the project and possible disbanding of the group. Conflict between individuals in a small group is very common, and may even be desirable (up to a point) in some instances (see Chapter 7 – section 7.5 on Groupthink). In what follows we will explore intragroup conflict in more detail and look at the causes and effects of conflict, types of conflict, how conflict may be managed and cultural differences.

Causes and effects of conflict

Conflict may broadly be defined as behaviour resulting from individual beliefs of group members that the goals of each cannot be achieved simultaneously (Pruitt and Rubin, 1986). These beliefs cause individual group members to recognise that their own goals or desired achievements may well be thwarted by others in the group. This leads to actions (verbal or physical) to oppose others with the result that conflict occurs. This is represented diagrammatically in Figure 5.3.

FIGURE 5.3 The development of conflict among members of a small group

TABLE 5.1 Some examples of organisational and interpersonal causes of conflict in small groups

Organisational or structural causes of conflict	Interpersonal causes of conflict
Competition over scarce or shared resources	Poor or faulty communications between group members
Uncertainty about what an individual or group is responsible for	Inappropriate and destructive rather than constructive criticism within the group
Interdependence of different groups for one group to perform effectively	Competition rather than co-operation between members of the group
Differential rewards given to group members	Poor leadership and/or power struggles and leadership challenges within the group
Power relationships	Individuals in powerful positions concerned to maintain their powerbase

Conflict can arise over a very wide range of issues including differences in attitudes and opinions, competition for scarce resources (see section 5.2.2 on Social dilemmas), power struggles and leadership challenges in a group, personality clashes between two people, status differentials and access to information. These may be categorised under one of two headings: organisational or structural causes and interpersonal causes. Table 5.1 shows some examples of each of these – I am sure you will be able to think of more.

Space restrictions preclude a detailed examination of each of the factors shown in Table 5.1; here we shall look in detail at one example of each category – differential rewards at an organisational level, and destructive rather than constructive criticism at an interpersonal level.

Kabanoff (1991) provides a useful analysis of the tension that exists in most organisations between *parity* and *equality*.

Parity relates to rewarding people or groups in relation to the contributions made and seniority of position in the organisation. Equality reflects the belief that everybody should be treated equally. Parity considerations are usually concerned with financial rewards, and equality considerations with socio-emotional aspects of working in an organisation, such as politeness, friendliness and feeling free to say what one thinks. Conflict between an individual or group in an organisation may arise from lack of equity when people think they are not paid enough or some people (for example, 'fat cat' executives) are overpaid. Conflict results from lack of equality if some people or groups feel they are not treated with respect, feel they are not able to speak freely and are treated in an unfriendly way.

The effects of conflict can be both negative and positive, but conflict generally has very strong negative connotations. We have seen obvious effects in the scenario at the beginning of this chapter. More subtle and often unnoticed effects are negative stereotyping of other individuals in the group, a group splitting into factions and a shift in leadership style from democratic to authoritarian (Fodor, 1976).

On the positive side, conflict makes people aware of different opinions and judgements that exist in the group. In addition, conflict may encourage individuals to want better to understand opposing opinions (but not if people are feeling defensive). Finally, as we shall see in Chapter 7 when considering groupthink, conflict at a moderate level may lead to better quality decision-making and enhance commitment to the decision the group finally agrees upon.

Conflict resolution

Here we will consider three different approaches to conflict resolution; the first looks at different individual styles people may adopt; the second has to do with people getting together to form coalitions within groups; the third is to escalate a conflict. Bargaining and negotiation is dealt with separately, since it is such an important and widely used strategy, in the next section of this chapter. Additional strategies are dealt with in a handbook by Deutsch and Coleman (2000).

When faced with a conflict between people in a small group, such as that outlined in the scenario at the beginning of this chapter, how do you think you would respond? More precisely, do you believe you have a preferred style for attempting to resolve different conflicts across a range of different situations? Thomas (1976; see also Blake and Mouton, 1970) suggested that there were five different individual styles which could be located across two general dimensions. The two dimensions are 'concern with the interests of others' and 'concern with self-interests'. The five styles are given below:

1 *accommodation* – allowing others to get what they want
2 *collaboration* – seeking to achieve the best outcomes for all involved
3 *compromise* – seeking to achieve outcomes which everybody has some agreement with
4 *competition* – trying to achieve the outcomes that reflect an individual's own interests
5 *avoidance* – denying that conflict exists or is present to such an extent that it is dysfunctional for the group.

Each of these five individual conflict resolution styles, apart from compromise, can be seen as high or low on each of the two general dimensions, as shown in Figure 5.4. A person's preferred style may be measured using a questionnaire developed by Rahim (1983).

Having identified these five different styles, is any one better than the others in terms of effective conflict resolution? It seems clear that both the avoidance and competition styles are not going to result in conflict resolution. Avoidance ignores the problem, and competition, at best, results in one individual view prevailing without agreement from others. Accommodation may leave the individual who has given up his or her views to others feeling dissatisfied. Collaboration and compromise seem the most effective from the point of view of potentially satisfying all or most

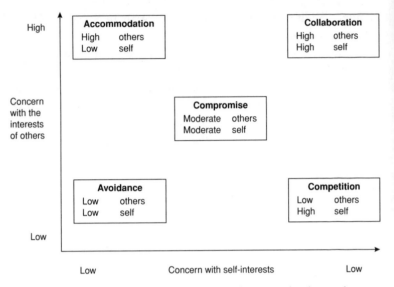

FIGURE 5.4 Five individual conflict resolution styles located along the two dimensions of 'concern for others' and 'concern for self'

Source: adapted from Thomas (1976)

of the members of the group and dealing with conflicts so that they do not rear up at a later date.

A different approach to conflict resolution is *coalition formation* which occurs when two or more group members form a subgroup and agree to co-operate to achieve mutually desired outcomes (Tesser, 1995). Coalitions are based solely on utility rather than liking between the individuals; this means that coalitions may be fragile and susceptible to collapse. The main factor which determines whether coalitions will work and endure revolves around commitment to achieving the desired outcomes. Where commitment is very high the coalition will survive in the face of obstacles, but where low it may stumble at the first hurdle. Another related factor is the extent to which coalition members are tempted to defect in order to join a different coalition.

Coalitions may help to resolve conflicts in small groups but do not have a lot of success in changing a competitive group into a co-operative one. Coalitions exclude some people in a group, and a number of coalitions may form within a group. When the latter happens, competition may develop between the coalitions and conflict be transferred from an individual to a subgroup level (Thibaut and Kelley, 1959).

Coalitions in organisational contexts tend to operate according to a small number of general principles. First, coalitions tend to happen more often with a very small group rather than a larger group. This may be because the rewards are greater for a small coalition and the fact that a large coalition, with a range of competing views in addition to areas of agreement, is more difficult to manage. In addition, ideological factors may make some coalitions more attractive to individuals than other coalitions (Miller and Komorita, 1986).

Coalitions may serve to reduce conflict in small groups; however, the very fact that a coalition will reflect areas of agreement and disagreement between individual members of the coalition means that conflicts may not be properly resolved. Having unresolved conflicts means that they re-emerge as more important when other objectives have been achieved by the group.

An approach to conflict resolution which seems counter-intuitive is to escalate the conflict. Such an approach has been called *escalative intervention* (Van der Vliert *et al.*, 1995), with the rationale that bringing matters to a head will present the group with very strong pressures to reach agreement. The approach also has the benefit of presenting a situation to group members who have been showing avoidance (see Figure 5.4). The advantages of escalation are that a clearer understanding of the issues may be obtained, as well as a deeper understanding of the different points of view held by individuals in the group. However, the strategy is a high-risk one since the outcome may be for the conflict to get out of control and for the group to break up because it is unworkable. There may also be ethical issues with conflict escalation; for example, long-term psychological harm may be present for some individuals. There is also deliberate manipulation of the group by one or more people within it (a coalition perhaps) or by outside forces. To manage conflict escalation requires great skill and understanding of people, and dynamics operating in small groups (Van der Vliert *et al.*, 1995). Generally, such an approach should be avoided unless few or no other alternatives present themselves, or other approaches have failed.

Negotiation and bargaining

Negotiation and bargaining is the most common and often the most successful approach to resolving intragroup (and intergroup) differences and conflict. Negotiation skills are seen as critical to the success of work groups and effective team-working. Negotiation may be defined as communications that take place between opposing sides (individuals in a group or different groups) in a conflict where offers and counter-offers are made until a solution is found on which both sides agree (Pruitt and Carnevale, 1993). Bargaining is different in the sense that both sides give up something in return for something else. In a legal setting plea-bargaining is where the defence and prosecution agree on a charge to which the defendant will plead guilty. The prosecution gives up pressing a more serious charge in exchange for the defence agreeing to the defendant pleading guilty. The defendant is thus guaranteed a lighter sentence because of the guilty plea to the lesser charge. The underlying principles of this legal example apply generally to a wide range of organisational and domestic situations where two sides are in dispute or conflict.

Two approaches to bargaining were identified over 30 years ago by Walton and McKersie (1965). These are *distributive bargaining* and *integrative bargaining*. They are defined as follows:

- Distributive bargaining is where a fixed sum of resources is divided up. It leads to win–lose outcomes between the two sides.
- Integrative bargaining is where both sides seek to maximise potential gains. It leads to win–win outcomes between the two sides.

Distributive bargaining is competitive in the sense that the gain made by one person in a group is at the expense of another losing.

For example, in worker–management bargaining over pay, a rise of £1 for the worker is a loss of £1 for management. Distributive bargaining does not properly resolve conflict since, for example, losers on one occasion will remember this and become determined to be winners on a future occasion. Over a period of time then, winners and losers may alternate between sides and, depending on the importance of what is lost, grudges or negative emotions may characterise the relationship between the two sides. It may be that some conflicts can only be resolved in this way; however, the integrative bargaining approach should first be tried since both sides potentially stand to gain.

Integrative bargaining assumes that disagreement or conflict can be resolved and that both parties or sides can reach agreement and a solution representing gains for each. Further advantages of successful integrative bargaining are that positive relationships between the two parties are fostered with the consequence that working together in the future is facilitated. For a small group, the benefits are that positive intragroup relations can be achieved, and the group as a whole can work together effectively and cohesively.

Pruitt *et al.* (1983) suggest five main strategies that often help integrative bargaining to be successful and win–win agreements to be reached between the two parties. These are summarised in Table 5.2.

Take the example of members of a small group attempting to reach internal agreement over whether or not to implement a 'green' environment policy in their company. Some group members think this is a good idea, others disagree and say there are other priorities to attend to at the moment. Using the strategy of non-specific compensation might result in those opposing the green policy being asked to identify a number of other priorities. Agreement on the implementation of the green policy could be reached by the group also agreeing to deal with one other priority which has been identified. The strategy of log-rolling might mean that those supporting introduction of the green policy identify areas of high value and low value within the policy. At the same time those wanting to deal with other priorities make the same assessment for their priorities. Areas of low priority from both sides are then not

TABLE 5.2 Strategies of bargaining that facilitate both sides reaching integrative agreements

Integrative strategy	Description
Broadening the pie	Additional resources are made available to enable both sides to achieve positive outcomes
Non-specific compensation	One side gets the outcome it wants, the other side receives compensation on a related matter of importance to that side
Log-rolling	Each side makes concessions on low priority matters in exchange for concessions on matters that are of higher priority
Cost-cutting	One side gets the outcome it wants while the other side has the costs of these outcomes reduced or eliminated
Bridging	Neither side obtains the outcomes they originally wanted, but a new set of outcomes is agreed that satisfies the interests of both sides

Source: adapted from Pruitt *et al*. (1983)

actioned and areas of high priority agreed upon to action. Both sides win and the group as a whole agrees how to move forward. A more complex version is for each side to make concessions on matters that are unimportant to one side but important to the other.

Integrative bargaining has obvious appeal since both sides stand to gain; however, finding win–win outcomes for both sides can prove extremely difficult (Ross and Ward, 1995). The dangers are that each side may not find out about the really important matters of the other side. In addition, the more a matter is of personal importance to one side, the more biased (negative) their perceptions of the other side. In more extreme circumstances, one side may come to regard the other as opponents and distrust whatever they say (Thompson, 1995).

On the positive side, however, where people do attempt to strive for integrative outcomes, research has shown that threats decrease and attempts to co-operate increase. Open exchange of information is also more likely to occur, and relationships between individuals develop more positively and in a friendly manner (Neale and Bazerman, 1991).

Cross-cultural differences

One of the key dimensions along which different cultures have been identified as varying is known as the individualistic–collectivistic dimension (Hofstede, 1980; Smith and Bond, 1998). *Individual-istic cultures* tend to value individual achievement over group achievement and individual rights and needs over collective rights and responsibilities. By contrast, *collectivistic cultures* tend to place great value on group achievements and emphasise collective needs and responsibilities over individual needs. In broad terms, western cultures such as the USA and Great Britain are classified as individualistic, and cultures such as Japan, China, and Taiwan as collectivistic.

Ting-Toomey *et al.* (1991) proposed that in the area of conflict resolution, parties in individualistic cultures would be more concerned with saving their own face or dignity when attempting to reach agreement. In contrast, collectivistic cultures would be more concerned with trying to save the face or dignity of the other side when attempting to resolve conflicts and disagreements. If you consider some of the conflict resolution styles we encountered in section 5.3.2 and the integrative bargaining strategy in section 5.3.3, what might you predict about these different types of cultures?

Ting-Toomey *et al.* (1991) predicted that individualistic cultures would tend to show greater preference for conflict resolution strategies that are dominant and integrative, and that collectivistic cultures would tend to use accommodating and avoidant styles more. To investigate these predictions researchers in five different

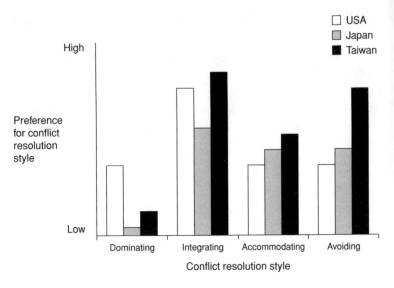

FIGURE 5.5 Conflict resolution styles exhibited by people from the USA, Japan and Taiwan

Source: adapted from Ting-Toomey *et al.* (1991)

countries asked nearly a thousand students to complete a questionnaire designed to ascertain the importance of saving their own face and the face of others in conflict situations.

As can be seen from Figure 5.5, students at university in the USA showed more of a preference for dominance in conflict resolution than did students from Japan or Taiwan. By contrast, students from Japan and Taiwan showed a stronger preference for both accommodation and avoidant conflict resolution styles than did students from the USA. This pattern of findings confirms the predictions made; however, caution is needed if one is attempting to generalise the results of real conflict situations and style of conflict resolution that people might actually have preferences for. This is because students were used and asked to complete a questionnaire; also, actual and real conflict situations were not investigated. What people say they will do in an imaginary situation often differs from what they actually do! Nevertheless, the research is valuable since it points out potential differences between cultures that are consistent with the idea of collectivistic and individualistic cultural differences.

Social influence

Individuals who interact in small groups often try to influence and change the attitudes, views and judgements of others in the group in order to arrive at a consensus, group view or decision. Small groups may sometimes develop factions within, where one faction may represent the majority and the other faction the minority. Where *majority influence* prevails, members of the group conform to the group norms. This is called *normative influence* because the pressure on dissenting individuals to conform to the views of others comes from not wanting to upset the group or cause conflict. When people conform they usually publicly agree with the rest of the group, but privately do not agree with the predominant view, judgement and so on. Here you get public compliance but not private acceptance. A second type of influence in a group is called *informational influence*, where individuals change their views privately as a result of new or different information that has been presented to them. Majority influence is most likely to occur as a result of normative influence.

When a faction in a group is in a minority (a minority of one at times!), it may succumb to majority group pressure and conform. However, minorities can also exert influence and change the views of the majority. Sometimes this comes about as a result of information influence, but other factors are also usually involved. In what follows we shall look in a little more detail at both majority and minority influence.

Majority influence

A classic and highly influential series of studies conducted by Asch (1951, 1955, 1956) demonstrated how majority group pressure could influence individuals to change their judgement. These experiments were based on presenting participants with an easy

 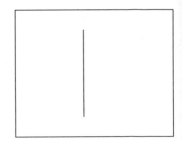

FIGURE 5.6 Typical example of a line judgement task used by Asch in his series of classic experiments

judgemental task involving first being presented with three different length lines and then another line the same length as one of the three original lines presented. The participants' task was simply to identify which of the three lines matched the standard line. Figure 5.6 provides an example of this line task – notice that as you look at the task on your own while reading this book how very easy and simple the judgement seems.

To investigate the effect of majority influence Asch recruited participants for the study and placed one participant in a room with seven other people. The participant was led to believe that these seven were also participants when, in fact, they were confederates of Asch. The group was presented with a series of line judgement tasks. On each trial, each member of the group had to say which line matched the standard line. Asch arranged things so that the real participant sat at the end of the row and answered last. A typical experiment would involve 18 trials, where on the first six trials the seven confederates gave the obviously correct answer (line (b)), but for the remaining 12 trials would give the same wrong answer (e.g. line (a) in Figure 5.6). Imagine you were sitting at the end of the row and heard all seven people give an obviously wrong answer. What would you do?

Asch found that of 123 participants in the above experimental set-up, just under 25 per cent gave the correct answer and were not influenced by the majority view. However, nearly 75 per cent gave at least one wrong answer from the 12 where the majority gave the wrong answer, and just over 60 per cent gave

three or more wrong answers. A small number of the 132 participants gave the wrong answer on all 12 occasions! Asch
interviewed participants at the end of the experiment. Those who
had given the wrong answer said they did so to avoid creating
disharmony or tension in the group because they did not want
to spoil the results of the experiment, and a few did so because
that was what they saw.

Factors affecting conformity

Numerous variations on this basic experiment were conducted by
Asch to determine conditions most and least likely to produce conformity through majority influence. Asch (1955) found that
conformity was reduced where one of the confederates gave the
correct answer (an 'ally') and where one of the confederates gave
a different wrong answer to the other confederates. If participants
felt the group to be attractive to belong to, conformity increased.
Stang (1972) found that people with high self-esteem succumbed
to majority influence less than those with low self-esteem. Bond
and Smith (1996) reported that collectivistic cultures are more
likely to conform to a majority view than individualistic cultures.
Of more relevance to interacting groups, perhaps, Lewis et al.
(1972) found that conformity was actually higher when participants were led to believe that the group would endure and there
would be opportunities for interaction with other group members.
Literally hundreds of studies have been conducted since Asch's
original experiments; these studies have mapped out in detail conditions where majority influence is more or less likely to result in
conformity.

Informational majority influence and conformity

Conformity resulting from majority influence, as detailed above, is
best explained by normative social influence. However, informational social influence may come into play at times. Baron et al.
(1996) demonstrated that judgements made when a task was difficult or more ambiguous than the line task of Asch were susceptible
to majority influence. When a task is perceived as difficult, people
are more likely to depend on the views of others since they would

be uncertain about their own judgements. This is believed to be important to the person making the judgement.

Generalisation

One drawback of much of the research on social influence is that while judgements are made by people in small groups, there is rarely opportunity for interaction and communication between group members. Hence no discussion can take place within the group to clarify and better understand why some people seem to be giving an obviously wrong answer. However, think back to experiences you have had working in small groups where somebody makes a suggestion. Nobody says anything and you privately disagree but say nothing. A group has often proceeded with the suggestion on the assumption that 'silence means consent'. Nevertheless, while studies on majority influence give us great insight into factors and processes involved, it does seem strange that the effect of discussion inside the group has not been carefully researched.

Minority influence

Under certain circumstances a minority view in a group will prevail and change the majority view. Moscovici (1985) was concerned that social psychologists had paid too much attention to majority influence and ignored historical examples of minority influence prevailing, in the end, over commonly accepted views in society. Examples, such as Galileo advocating that the Earth was not at the centre of the universe; Darwin and evolution; and Freud and the unconscious, come to mind. In each case a minority, and initially rejected or discredited view, prevailed in the face of an overwhelming majority. Moscovici (1985) was interested to discover the conditions under which minorities have influence over the majority.

Three main factors seem to be involved. First, the minority must show a behaviour style which is consistent – this is defined by Mugny *et al.* (1984) as a firm, systematic, coherent and autonomous repetition of the same view or judgement. The minority must not waver in their view or change their mind. Second, the minority should not be perceived by the majority as rigid or dogmatic, but must produce good arguments and some evidence, where possible, to support their case. Essentially, the minority must seek to persuade the majority and provide new information or information in a different way to encourage them to change their minds. In addition, some flexibility needs to be shown by the minority and some concessions, but not the central ones, made to the majority (Mugny *et al.*, 1984). Third, the general social context may be important – arguing a minority position along the lines of current social trends is more likely to be influential than arguing in the opposite direction.

Minority influence is therefore different to majority influence in that the latter produces conformity through normative social influence. Minority influence is more likely to produce personal acceptance or agreement as a result of informational influence. An additional explanation put forward by Nemeth (1995) is that minorities, compared with majorities, expend a great deal of cognitive effort and systematic thought when presenting their views. Thus the minority will put a lot of effort into understanding the arguments and views of the majority to see where there are weaknesses, lack of evidence and so on. In so doing, the minority encourage the majority to think about arguments or explanations that the majority may not have thought about. Once minority influence has prevailed over the majority the whole group becomes committed and believes in the one minority point of view. This often does not happen with majority influence since people may conform in order not to 'rock the boat' but privately believe something different, as we saw with the Asch experiments.

Overview

Returning to the scenario described at the start of this chapter, I am sure you can think of numerous times when you have worked or interacted socially in small groups and conflict has arisen. Think of one or two examples that you can recall clearly. What were the causes of the conflict and how, if at all, was the conflict resolved? It might have been through co-operation for the good of the group where your own personal interests took second place. Alternatively, a compromise might have been reached which met the differences half-way. Another approach might have been the minority simply agreeing to adopt the majority position for the sake of harmony in the group and so that the group could get on with the task it had been set. Finally, you might have been in a minority, stuck to your guns, and persuaded the majority round to your point of view. As you can see from reading this chapter, there is a wide range of ways in which conflict can be dealt with and resolved. In most real-life situations it is likely that conflict resolution is achieved through employing a number of different strategies or approaches at the same time. The theory and research presented in this chapter focused on specific strategies so that each could be explored in more detail.

Summary

Co-operation and conflict occur in all small groups. When conflict develops within the group a degree of resolution is needed; otherwise conflict may escalate and threaten the continuation of the group. Co-operation and competition in groups has been researched through the prisoner's dilemma and social dilemmas. Each explores when individuals act in their own self-interest and when for the mutual good of others. Conflict may be defined as behaviour resulting from individual beliefs of group members that the goals of each cannot be achieved. Conflict resolution styles include accommodation, collaboration, compromise, competition and avoidance. Conflict may be resolved through coalition formation – where two or more group members work together to achieve mutually desired outcomes. Coalitions may be fragile, reflecting both areas of agreement and disagreement.

There are two main approaches to bargaining – distributive bargaining (win–lose outcomes) and integrative bargaining (win–win outcomes). Integrative bargaining, when achieved, fosters commitment to decisions taken and enhances interpersonal relationships in groups. Individualistic cultures show preferences for conflict resolution that are dominant and integrative, collectivistic cultures show preferences for accommodating or avoidant conflict resolution. Social influence in a group may be achieved through majority or minority influence. Majority influence produces conformity mainly through normative influence. Minority influence is achieved through a consistent behavioural style and the production of good arguments for a position with a good understanding of the opposing positions. Conflict resolution in real life often demonstrates use of a number of strategies simultaneously.

Further reading

Witte, E. and Davis, J. H. (eds) (1996) *Understanding Group Behaviour: Consensual Action by Small Groups,* Hillsdale, NJ: Erlbaum. A collection of papers written by experts and leaders in the field. Provides detailed follow-up to some of the issues raised in this chapter.

Weeks, D. (1992) *The Eight Essential Steps to Conflict Resolution,* New York: Putnam. A practically based book dealing with a wide range of interpersonal conflicts. Looks at why conflicts arise and how to deal with them on both interpersonal and emotional levels.

Thompson, L. (1998) *The Mind and Heart of the Negotiator,* Upper Saddle River, NJ: Prentice-Hall. A readable, short text that provides further insights into bargaining from a social psychological perspective. Up-to-date and accessible.

Fisher, R. and Urg. U. (1991) *'Getting to Yes'. Negotiating Agreement Without Giving In* (3rd edn), London: Business Books. Practical tips and advice about negotiation.

Leadership

Introduction

WHO DO YOU REGARD AS really great leaders? Names
that often come to mind are Mahatma Gandhi, Nelson
Mandela, Winston Churchill, and Margaret Thatcher – all political leaders. Often infamous names come to mind such as Adolf
Hitler and Pol Pot. However, for you, great leaders may not be
politicians at all but people associated with sport, such as Sir Alex
Ferguson, the manager of Manchester United football club. Some
leaders are visionaries, others use their position of power, and
others persuade us to do what they want. In all this it is not difficult to see that leaders are very important and influential people
who may be responsible for creating enormous change in our
lives. You will not be surprised to learn, in light of this, that
the study of leadership has occupied a central position in social
psychology for over 50 years and is an important area of interest
for organisational psychology (Greenberg and Baron, 1993). In this
chapter we will explore a wide range of approaches, including
personality, behavioural style and leadership effectiveness, that
represent both past and recent interests of social psychologists. We
conclude the chapter by considering gender and cultural differences
in leadership.

Basics of leadership

Before considering different theoretical approaches to leadership
we need to set a context of understanding what leadership is, the
relationship between leaders and followers, and how leaders are
chosen or emerge.

Leadership as social influence

It seems trite to say that leaders are leaders of people; however, a leader can only lead if other people are prepared to do or say what is required. Yukl (1994) provides a useful definition of leadership as 'the process through which one member of a group (its leader) influences other group members towards the attainment of specific group goals'. Three important features emerge from this definition. First, that leadership is about how a person exerts social influence to get other people in the group to do what he or she wants. Second, the leader is a member of a group, and to be effective must be recognised and accepted as the leader of the group by the others. A leader who does not gain recognition and acceptance from the rest of the group will be able to lead only through using the power he or she has (see section 6.2.2) or through coercion. If the leader has no power he or she is unlikely to be able to continue in the role. Third, leadership is about the attainment of group goals, and to be effective the goals of the leader should coincide with the goals of the rest of the group. Ideally, group goals should be agreed in advance and have the commitment of all the members of the group. You may be able to think of examples where this is not the case, such as the Cabinet of the government, when ministers disagree with the Prime Minister or other Cabinet ministers. The resignation of Margaret Thatcher as Prime Minister in 1989 exemplifies this well.

Leadership may be regarded as social influence; however, leaders occupy powerful positions in a group. There are different types of power that a leader may possess or use and it is to this that we now turn.

Leadership as power

The most enduring and respected analysis of power is that provided by French and Raven (1959), and updated by Raven (1993). This analysis shows that there are six types of power: reward power, referent power, informational power, legitimate power, expert power and coercive power. *Reward power* is demonstrated when the leader is able to influence others by providing what they want, such as promotion or increased salary, and taking away what they do not want, such as poor equipment or poor office working conditions. Note that this type of power can only work if the leader is able to offer such rewards. When leaders promise what they are not empowered to reward, relationships with the other group members or the followers may well deteriorate.

Referent power is manifested when the leader is respected and looked up to by other group members; the leader emphasises the identity of the group for the members and acts as a role model to provide a sense of common identity. Effective use of referent power makes group members want to be part of a team and not be seen to let anybody down. If the leader loses respect from the other group members, referent power will diminish.

Informational power occurs where the leader may have privileged access to information he or she uses in a logical argument to persuade other members of the group. This type of power is effective to the extent that serious faults cannot be found with the position the leader is arguing for.

Legitimate power means that other members of the group accept that the leader has the right to influence them, and uses their status, hierarchies and established rules and norms to this end. Legitimate power is usually formal as in, for example, the army or police with their officer hierarchies. Legitimate power disappears as soon as the formal position occupied has been removed, for example, demotion of an officer to the ranks.

Expert power comes from the leader having a high level of knowledge or recognised superior ability in a specialised area. The media often uses experts such as professors to comment on a matter because we are likely to believe a person who is a recognised expert in his or her field. In today's fast-changing world, experts have to keep up-to-date or they will not be seen as credible.

Coercive power is shown when a leader has the ability to threaten and/or punish group members if they do not conform to the leader's wishes. Use of this kind of power usually produces negative feelings in people, but, where the punishment may involve death or imprisonment, use of this power often results in group members obeying the leader. Notable exceptions come to mind, such as Nelson Mandela's fight for democracy in South Africa and the 25 years he spent in prison for never giving up on the vision he had for the black people of his country.

These six types of power may all be used at different times by one leader, or a leader may rely almost exclusively on one or two types of power. Table 6.1 summarises these six types of power and provides a leadership example of each.

Given that these six types of power may be available to a leader, it is of interest to discover when each is most likely to be used. Where a group of people or a nation come to agree increasingly less with the policies and behaviours of their leaders, the use of coercive power may begin to dominate. For example, Adolf Hitler and the Nazis relied almost entirely on coercive power in their brutal and calculated slaughter of three million Jews during the Second World War. In an organisational setting, Frost and Stahelski (1988) investigated the extent to which middle and senior managers used the six types of power. As can be seen from Figure 6.1, senior managers tend to use coercive, reward and legitimate power more than do middle managers. Note that both types of managers used referent and expert power most frequently and to about the same extent. Stahelski *et al.* (1989), in a follow-up study, showed that the more senior a manager becomes in an organisation the more he or she is likely to use coercive, reward and referent power.

This analysis of power in relation to leadership provides insights into how a leader influences others to think or behave in ways he or she wishes them to; however, such an analysis does not tell us about what type of people, if there is a type, become leaders, how leaders are effective and the way in which different situations may suit different types of leaders. We will return to these themes later in the chapter, but we now go on to consider leaders and followers.

TABLE 6.1 The six types of power suggested by French and Raven (1959) and Raven (1993)

Type of Power	Description	Example
Reward power	Ability of the leader to provide what others want or remove what they dislike or do not want.	Manager in organisation has the power to promote a worker and/or give higher salary.
Referent power	Respect with which the leader is held by group members and ability to create common sense of identity.	Role model, such as the Queen. Power maintained as long as the person commands respect.
Informational power	Use of information, which may be privileged to the leader, in a logical way to present compelling argument.	Chief executive of a company knows there will be a take-over bid since only he or she has been working on this with another company executive.
Legitimate power	Group members accept rules and norms of the leader and regard leader as properly occupying the position.	The Prime Minister is democratically elected by voters in Britain and seen to legitimately occupy the position.
Expert power	Leader perceived and regarded as having superior knowledge and/or ability in a specialist field.	Professor of psychology is seen to be a specialist in the field, but note usually in a selected area.
Coercive power	Leader has the ability to threaten and punish others to get his or her own way.	Dictators, such as Hitler, maintain power through punishment.

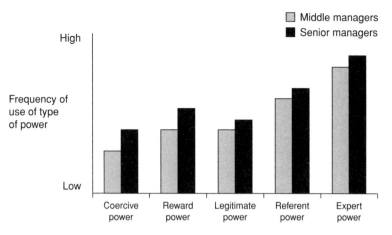

FIGURE 6.1 Use of five types of power by middle and senior managers

Source: adapted from Frost and Stahelski (1988)

Leaders and followers

The main focus of this chapter is naturally on leaders, but we should not lose sight of the people that are led – the followers. Looking at leadership as social influence and the use leaders make of different types of power fails to capture the reciprocal influence that followers have on leaders. We will see later in this chapter that leaders need to be sensitive to the needs of followers and may treat group members differently, depending on situational factors and the nature of the task facing the group (see Fiedler's contingency theory of leadership – section 6.5.1). Lee (1991) argues that a complex relationship exists between leaders and followers where there has to be give-and-take by both. Furthermore, Lee (1991) claims that effective followers are essential for effective leadership; here effective followers are those who are enthusiastic, committed and self-reliant. Senge (1990) goes so far as to assert that organisations which are able continuously to respond to change and to learn about the needs of their customers are characterised by leaders, such as chief executives, empowering the workers in the organisation. This means that workers at all levels in a company must feel that they are part of the decision-making process. If they do feel this, Senge (1990) claims that employees will be committed, perform at high levels and enjoy high morale – features that Senge regards as essential for any organisation to be successful and continue to be successful in an ever-changing environment.

According to Lee (1991), followers may be crudely put into one of four categories according to whether or not they are active or passive and high or low in critical thinking. The four categories, as shown in Figure 6.2, are *yes people*, *sheep*, *alienated followers* and *effective followers*. From what we have considered above in relation to Senge's view of organisational success, one key task of a leader is to create effective followers.

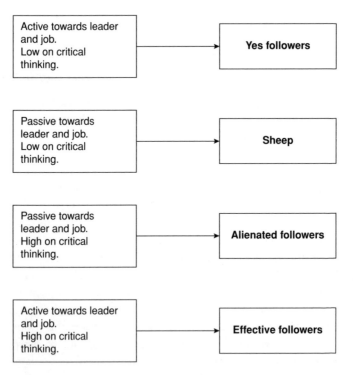

FIGURE 6.2 Four types of followers suggested by Lee (1991). Note that effective followers are desirable and will challenge the leader

Choosing a leader

Leaders achieve their position by a variety of means. In democratic countries political leaders receive the support of the people from the votes cast. In contrast, dictators may achieve their position through a military coup. Some leaders inherit their position, for example, the Queen and hereditary peers in Britain. In many organisational settings, leaders, such as chief executives, are appointed on the basis of ability, experience and often their visionary qualities (see Transformational leadership – section 6.6).

Leaders who achieve their position from people who vote for them are often those who create a sense of emotional comfort in the voters (Kinder and Sears, 1985), and express high levels of optimism about the future of the country to the voters (Zallow and Seligman, 1990).

Personality and leadership

At the start of this chapter you were invited to think about people you regard as great leaders. As a little exercise, think about two of these people again and write a short description of each. If you analyse this description, there will no doubt be personality traits present. This focus on personality traits reflects the long-standing approach of psychologists to seeking personality traits or characteristics that set great leaders apart from other people. This is often referred to as the *great person theory* and the idea that certain people are born leaders because of the characteristics they inherit. The approach therefore relies on two assumptions: first, that a small number of defining personality characteristics are associated with exceptional leaders; second, that such characteristics are inherited, not learned through socialisation and experience. Unfortunately, empirical evidence has failed to provide strong support for either claim, but especially the idea that leaders possess certain special personality traits (Stogdill, 1974).

Mann (1959) conducted a review of over 100 studies which had attempted to correlate different personality traits with leadership. Only weak evidence was found for leaders possessing the traits of intelligence, extraversion, dominance and sensitivity to others. It was also found that leaders tend to be slightly taller than average. This may reflect the finding that we choose leaders who fit our stereotype of a leader (Eagly and Karau, 1991). Hence people who occupy important or 'big' jobs may fit with a stereotype that 'size matters', i.e. they are taller than the average person. Mullen *et al.* (1989) suggest that only two traits seem to offer a correlation with leadership; these are intelligence and talkativeness. Talkativeness is an interesting trait in this context – just because a person talks a lot does not necessarily mean what is said is valuable or relevant. However, Mullen *et al.* (1989) suggest that people perceive talkativeness as a trait associated with leadership because the act of talking a lot makes the person more salient or prominent in a group.

The traditional approach of attempting to associate certain personality traits with leaders has generally lost favour for five main reasons. First, there are many different personality traits that could be used to compare leaders with non-leaders but no agreement over which may be the central ones. Second, the trait approach does not take account of the situation or context in which the leader is operating. The approach assumes that a good leader in one situation would also make a good leader in a different situation; this is often not the case. Third, the focus on the idea that a group possesses just one leader is often incorrect. As we shall see in the next section, small groups are often characterised by the presence of two leaders. Fourth, the focus on the person rather than the situation may be an example of the *fundamental attribution error* (Ross, 1977). This is a well-evidenced error people make when attributing the causes of behaviour to a person. Attribution researchers consistently report that people over-emphasise personality factors and under-emphasise the social situation in which the behaviour takes place – especially if they are at some distance from the person (e.g. only a minority of the population are personally acquainted with the Prime Minister). Fifth and finally, the great person theory cannot predict in advance who will become a leader; most of the research takes place after the event and analyses characteristics of existing leaders.

In spite of these problems, there has been a recent revival of interest in the trait approach from work by Kirkpatrick and Locke (1991). Drawing upon both traditional personality traits and characteristics representing knowledge and experience, Kirkpatrick and Locke (1991) suggest that *successful* leaders possess eight important characteristics, which are summarised in Table 6.2. Some are ones you might expect to see, others need some explanation. Leadership motivation reflects the desire of the leader to lead and influence other people to achieve shared goals. Flexibility concerns the ability of the leader to notice changing circumstances and adaptively to respond as appropriate. Zaccaro *et al.* (1991) showed that the greater the degree of flexibility shown by a leader in a small group, the higher were the ratings of leadership ability attributed to the leader by other members of the group. Kirkpatrick and Locke (1991) do regard successful leaders as different from other

TABLE 6.2 Characteristics of successful leaders suggested by Kirkpatrick and Locke (1991)

Trait or characteristic	Description
Drive	Individual's desire or need to achieve, level of ambition, desire to succeed
Honesty and integrity	Trustworthiness, reliability, openness
Leadership motivation	Desire to influence other people and achieve shared outcomes and goals of the group
Self-confidence	Trust in leadership abilities
Cognitive ability	Intelligence, ability to deal with complex and large amounts of information
Knowledge of the business	Depth and breadth of understanding of the business and economic context
Creativity	Original thinking, visionary thinking
Flexibility	Ability to respond and adapt as situations change

people, and point out that the ability to cope with great responsibility and high pressures is a defining feature. Note that this approach is based on *successful* leaders and it is open to debate what criteria might be used to determine if a person is or is not a successful leader.

Behavioural style

Another way in which psychologists can remain focused on the individual while paying much less attention to psychological constructs such as traits or personality characteristics is to look at the actual behaviours performed by leaders. This approach has been much more productive over a long period of time and remains of contemporary importance.

Research on the *behavioural style* of leaders dates back at least 50 years to the ground-breaking research of Hemphill (1950). Hemphill conducted a study in which a large number of people rated the behaviour of leaders on a thousand different aspects. Statistical analysis revealed two main behavioural dimensions: group-centred and directive behaviours. Group-centred or 'consideration' behaviours are those shown by a leader considering interpersonal relationships in the group, developing a sense of trust between group members and generally looking after the emotional well-being of group members. By contrast, directive behaviours, often referred to as 'initiating structure', are more related to the task the group faces and include performance measures, allocating tasks to group members, ensuring norms and rules are upheld and ensuring that the role of the leader is understood among the group members. In short, consideration refers to leader behaviour which is sensitive to the social and emotional needs of group members, whereas initiating structure refers to behaviour concerned with group performance and achieving group goals.

Stogdill (1974), while at Ohio State University, characterised these two behavioural styles as two independent dimensions with each along a high–low continuum. It might seem that if a leader is high on one dimension then that person will be low on the other dimension. However, this seems not to be the case and a leader can be high or low on both dimensions, moderate on both dimensions, or high on one and low on the other. This raises the question of whether one combination is best and results in effective leadership. Perhaps not surprisingly, it seems that leaders who are high on both dimensions, or can be trained to be so, lead teams that achieve high levels of performance (Blake and Mouton, 1985). This was empirically supported in a study conducted by Tjosvold (1984). Here male and female student participants worked with each other, in pairs, on a problem with an assigned leader. The leader was an accomplice of the experimenter, and behaved in one of four ways: either showing high concern or low concern with productivity, together with either warmth or coldness towards the pair working on the task. After the first problem had been solved, the leader set the pair of participants a second problem but left them to solve it on their own. Tjosvold (1984) predicted that participant pairs would work hardest after experiencing a leadership style representing high productivity concerns with warmth towards the workers. This was indeed found, together with the participant pairs liking this leadership style the most and wanting to work with the leader in the future.

The behavioural styles of initiating structure and consideration are similar to those discovered by Bales and Slater (1955) using the technique of Interaction Process Analysis, which we looked at in Chapter 2. Interaction Process Analysis showed that in small problem-solving groups, two leadership roles emerged – the task leader and the socio-emotional leader. In contrast to Stogdill, Bales and Slater (1955) claimed that different people occupied these leadership roles. Inasmuch as one's position on either of the two dimensions (task or social) does not particularly predict one's position on the other dimension, it is unlikely – especially as group size increases – that the same person will happen to be the highest scorer on both dimensions. While there may be disagreement over whether one leader can or cannot occupy these two roles, these two dimensions of leadership style do seem fundamental, and have been found to apply in many different contexts (business, military and sport) and in different cultures (Bass, 1990).

A different approach to studying the behavioural style of leaders is represented by the highly influential and classic study by Lippett and White (1943). These researchers investigated the effects of three leadership styles – autocratic, democratic and laissez-faire – on group productivity, group atmosphere and how well group members or followers liked their leader. This research was conducted using adult leaders with schoolboys working on tasks such as making models from bars of soap. Figure 6.3 describes each leadership style and presents the effects on the groups of schoolboys. As may be seen, the democratic style of leadership does well across the board. Criticisms have been made of this study because the researchers themselves favoured democratic leadership, the research was conducted using schoolboys performing artificial

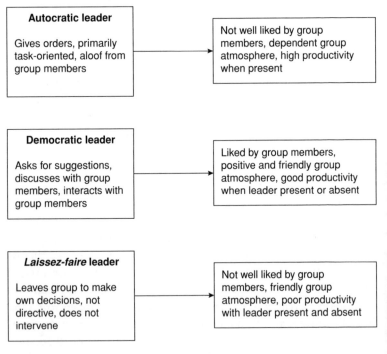

FIGURE 6.3 Three leadership styles studied by Lippett and White (1943) with effects on productivity, group atmosphere and liking for the leader

tasks, and the leaders were confederates of the researchers and hence role-playing the different styles of leadership. Nevertheless, these leadership behavioural styles do seem to reflect real-life leadership behaviour.

More recent research by Muczyk and Reimann (1987) has given added sophistication to the three leadership styles of Lippett and White (1943) by proposing two independent dimensions. These are autocratic–democratic and directive–permissive, and four leadership styles can be characterised using these two dimensions:

1 *Permissive democrats* – encourage participative decision-making, and allow group members high degree of autonomy.

2 *Permissive autocrats* – leader makes decision and allows group members high degree of autonomy in carrying out tasks.

3 *Directive democrats* – encourage participative decision-making, and closely monitor and control work of group members.

4 *Directive autocrats* – leader makes decisions, and closely monitors and controls work of group members.

All four styles of leadership seem to have their advantages (Greenberg and Baron, 1993), and successful leadership style seems to depend upon the organisational context and nature of the task facing the group. For example, directive autocrats may be successful when faced with an inexperienced group or where group members are hostile towards the organisation. By contrast, permissive autocrats may be successful when working with a group of technically highly skilled people who need to be left alone to get on with their individual specialist tasks. This reflects the importance of situational and task factors and how this may interact with the behavioural style of a leader. We explore such an interaction more fully below.

Leadership effectiveness

Theory and research on personality and behavioural style of a leader has regarded leadership effectiveness to be of central concern. In this section we look at three approaches which seek to discover what makes an effective leader and how different situations in which the group operates may determine whether one type of leader is effective or ineffective.

Fiedler's contingency theory

Fiedler's (1965, 1971, 1981) *contingency theory of leadership* draws on Bales' finding that small groups often have two leaders – a task-oriented leader and a socio-emotional leader. In order to predict leadership effectiveness Fiedler stated that an assessment of situational favourableness also had to be made. For Fiedler, leadership effectiveness is contingent, or depends upon, the behavioural style and whether the situation is favourable or unfavourable. Specifically, task-oriented leaders are most effective in highly favourable or unfavourable situations, while socio-emotional leaders are most effective in moderately favourable or more ambiguous situations. To understand this more fully, we need to look at how Fiedler determined leadership style and situational favourableness.

Fiedler developed what has come to be a well-known measure of leadership style through the Least Preferred Co-worker Scale (LPC). The LPC scale asks a leader to think about a person whom he or she found it difficult to work with or was able to work with least well. The scale uses 16 bipolar adjectives each with an 8 point scale; some examples are as follows:

pleasant	☐☐☐☐☐☐☐☐	unpleasant
friendly	☐☐☐☐☐☐☐☐	unfriendly
warm	☐☐☐☐☐☐☐☐	cold
interesting	☐☐☐☐☐☐☐☐	boring

| efficient | | | | | | | | | inefficient |
| co-operative | | | | | | | | | unco-operative |

Leaders who generally show a positive attitude to their LPC are categorised as socio-emotional leaders, while those who show a negative attitude to their LPC are task-oriented leaders. You may wish to get an indication of the type of leader you might be by thinking of a person whom you have found it difficult (or less easy) to work with and then rating that person by placing a tick in one of the boxes for each of the six bipolar adjectives given above. Once you have done this, use a scale of 1 to 8, with 1 on the extreme left and 8 on the extreme right. Scores can range from 8 to 48, with a low score indicating a socio-emotional leader and a high score a task-oriented leader.

Fiedler (1978) originally used a second measure to determine leadership style called the Assumed Similarity between Opposites scale (ASO). On this scale leaders are asked to think about two people – their most and least preferred co-workers. Using a number of bipolar adjectives as with the LPC scale, people showing a large difference in their views towards the least and most preferred co-workers are task-oriented, and those showing little difference are socio-emotional-oriented. Fiedler dropped the ASO scale because he found that the LPC scale was a more reliable and valid predictor of leadership style.

To assess the *situation*, Fiedler used three indicators as follows:

1 Leader–follower relationships. Categorised as good or poor.
2 The task structure – whether the task set the group was clear and unambiguous or unclear. Categorised as high or low.
3 Position of power of the leader – whether or not the leader has authority over the other members in the group. Categorised as strong or weak.

Since these three situational factors are each classified as a dichotomy, eight different situations are described as a result, and an overall assessment of situational favourableness (favourable, moderate or unfavourable) is made. Finally, Fiedler predicted that task-oriented leaders would be most effective in highly favourable situations (I, II, III in Table 6.3) and unfavourable situations (VII and VIII), while socio-emotional leaders would be effective in moderately favourable situations (IV, V and VI).

The logic behind this is that unfavourable situations require a leader to give clear guidance and direction to establish the nature of the task and how it may be accomplished. In highly favourable situations relationships between members are good and the task is clear, thus allowing a task-oriented leader to concentrate and be successful in achieving the group goal. Moderately favourable situations require a leader to support group members in order to improve interpersonal relationships so that the group can then move on to deal with the task that has been set. Fiedler found that leader–follower relationships are the most important situational factors in moderately favourable situations.

Thirty years of research on Fiedler's contingency theory has produced a good deal of empirical support. For example, Strube and Garcia (1981) conducted a meta-analytic review of over 170 studies and generally found strong support for the theory. However, Peters *et al.* (1985) reviewed both laboratory and field studies and found much less support for the theory from the latter type of research.

An interesting test of contingency theory was conducted in a field setting by Chemers *et al.* (1985). Here university management staff completed the LPC scale and were categorised as either task-oriented or socio-emotional leaders; at the same time the researchers classified their jobs as either situationally favourable, moderate or unfavourable. Having done this the levels of stress experienced by these staff was also measured. One would predict from contingency theory that task-oriented leaders would experience most stress in moderately favourable conditions, and socio-emotional leaders most stress in highly favourable or unfavourable situations. As Figure 6.4 shows, this is what the researchers found. Caution should be exercised in generalising these results since the way in which the situation was classified was largely subjective, and it is not clear that university managers are leaders. Chemers

TABLE 6.3 Fiedler's contingency theory of leadership effectiveness, showing type of leader predicted to be effective in each of the eight situations

	I	II	III	IV	V	VI	VII	VIII
Leader–follower relationships	Good	Good	Good	Good	Poor	Poor	Poor	Poor
Task structure	High	High	Low	Low	High	High	Low	Low
Leader's position of power	Strong	Weak	Strong	Weak	Strong	Weak	Strong	Weak
Overall situational favourableness	Very high	High	High	Moderate	Moderate	Moderate to low	Low	Very low
Style of leader for effectiveness	Task-oriented	Task-oriented	Task-oriented	Socio-emotional	Socio-emotional	Socio-emotional	Task-oriented	Task-oriented

Source: adapted from Fiedler (1978)

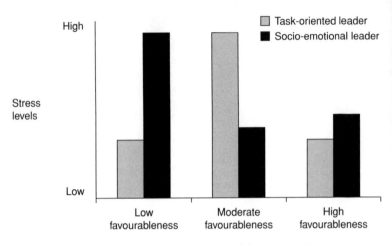

FIGURE 6.4 Levels of stress experienced by university managers in relation to leadership style and situational favourableness

Source: adapted from Chemers *et al*. (1985)

(1993) extended earlier findings by showing that leader–follower relationships and task performance were negatively affected by a wrong match between type of leader and type of situation.

A number of criticisms have been made of Fiedler's theory. First, the LPC scale may not provide a stable measure of leadership style since administering the scale twice to the same person over a relatively short period of time produces different scores and leadership classifications (Rice, 1978). In addition, as leaders become more experienced they may change their style and adapt to different situations quite well. Second, the three components of situational favourableness are each quite difficult to assess, and while Fiedler claims that leader–follower relationships are the most important of the three, this may not always be the case, and it is difficult and quite complex to be able to predict the relative importance of each of these three components in different situations. Finally, field studies, as mentioned earlier, have provided less support for the theory and have at times produced results opposite to those predicted by the theory (Peters *et al.*, 1985).

An overall evaluation of the theory does suggest that it has given us greater insight into leadership effectiveness and occupies a dominant position in the study of leadership. Refinement of the LPC scale and objective means of assessing situational favourableness is required. In addition, more research in 'real-life' applied settings is needed to tease out other variables better to explain the relative lack of support from research in the field.

Normative theory

One of the key tasks faced by any leader is that of decision-making; and when working with a small group of people one matter that Fiedler's contingency theory is silent about concerns the extent to which the followers or other group members should participate in decision-making. Put crudely, should the leader be autocratic and make decisions without consultation and involvement of other group members, or should the leader reach a decision through participation and consensus? This is at the heart of Vroom and Yelton's (1973) *normative theory* of leadership. Vroom and Yelton suggest three basic styles of leadership decision-making as follows:

1	*Autocratic*	–	leader makes decisions unilaterally and without follower participation or involvement.
2	*Consultative*	–	leader consults with group members and then makes decision unilaterally.
3	*Group decision*	–	leader consults and seeks views of other group members and reaches decision by consensus.

According to Vroom and Yelton, no one approach is best and leadership effectiveness is contingent upon two main situational factors: the extent to which a high-quality decision is required, and the extent to which it is important that the other group members accept the decision that is made. For example, if it is important that a high-quality decision is made but the leader does not have enough information upon which to base the decision, and it is important that the group members accept and are committed to the decision; then either the consultative or group decision style will be most effective. If there is limited time available for the leader to make the decision, then the consultative style will be the most appropriate. Take a different set of circumstances. If the leader believes for good reasons that the other group members do not have the knowledge or experience to make the right decision and the group will act on the decision made, the autocratic style of leadership will be most effective.

The model of leadership effectiveness is normative since Vroom and Yelton provide a complex set of rules – too elaborate and detailed to present here – to guide leaders in deciding which style of leader-participation (from the three given above) should be adopted. Vroom and Jago (1978) have updated the model and added two more decision-making styles on the continuum from highly autocratic to highly participative.

This model, while complex and requiring a computer program to work out the best leader decision-making style, has proved attractive in organisations and particularly with senior managers. The model's strengths are that it takes account of followers or other group members, and suggests that a leader is able to change his or her style of decision-making to suit different circumstances. However, there are shortcomings. For example, Heilman *et al.* (1984) found that managers preferred a participative style even when the model recommended an autocratic style. In addition, followers prefer a participative style of leadership on nearly all occasions while leaders will use autocratic styles at times. Finally, leaders facing a high-conflict situation between group members may revert to an autocratic style, against the model, because they are unable to manage the conflict that exists in the group.

Path–goal theory

The third contingency model of leadership effectiveness is that developed by House and Baetz (1979) which characterises the role of a leader to ensure that the group progresses along an appropriate path in order to achieve its goals. The *path–goal theory* of leadership suggests that leaders may adopt one of four styles while at the same time taking account of two contingency or situational factors. These are the characteristics of the followers and the environment in which the group is working. The four leadership styles are:

1 *Directive*   – the leader provides clear guidance, lets followers know what is expected of them, and produces work schedules.
2 *Supportive*   – the leader establishes good relationships with followers and shows concern for their needs.
3 *Participative*   – the leader consults with followers and encourages them to be involved in decision-making.
4 *Achievement-oriented* – the leader sets challenging goals and seeks improvement in follower performance.

The characteristics of the followers that the leader takes into account are about their level of experience, expertise and perceived ability. The work environment is concerned with how well structured the task is, whether the task is routine or unusual, and the formal authority system or organisational context in which the group is working. Figure 6.5 represents how all these different factors and leadership styles come together to produce outcomes for the group that are related both to performance on the task set and satisfaction among the group members.

Path–goal theory predicts that when a task is unstructured the best leadership style is likely to be directive. Where the followers are all highly skilled and experienced, a supportive style will be most effective. On a more emotional level, followers who have a high need for affiliation (to be with others and to get on with them) will do best with a supportive or participative style of leadership. People with a high need for achievement will prefer an achievement-oriented leader.

Good empirical support has been forthcoming for path–goal theory (Schriesham and De Nisi, 1981; Wofford and Liska, 1993). Its strength, as with normative theory, is its focus on followers and

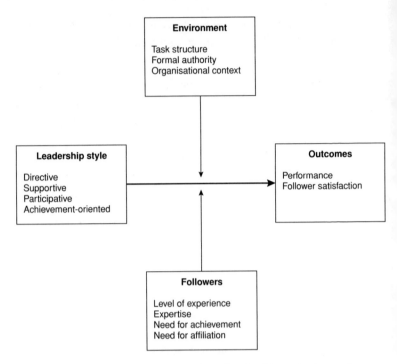

FIGURE 6.5 Path–goal theory: how leadership style is contingent upon environmental and follower factors to produce both performance and satisfaction outcomes for group members

the role of their participation in decision-making and performance at tasks.

In this section we have considered three theories of leadership effectiveness that are all based on a contingency approach. Both normative theory and path–goal theory have enjoyed wide application because of the consideration they give to leader--follower participation in group tasks. Fiedler's contingency model has probably been the most influential since the relationship between leadership style and situational factors underpins the other two models we have considered here. All three integrate aspects of personality, behavioural style and situational factors together to predict leadership effectiveness. These models have enjoyed wide application and success, and will continue to do so in the future through further refinement and research.

Transformational leadership

At the start of this chapter some examples of exceptional leaders were given – Winston Churchill, Nelson Mandela and so on. No doubt you can think of many more such as Martin Luther King and Margaret Thatcher. These leaders are regarded as exceptional and as agents of social, political, and economic change. These leaders are *transformational* in that they inspired people to change. With the rapid development of the internet, electronic commerce and the globalisation of companies, Bass (1997) claims that the value and need for transformational leadership will increase in the future. Transformational leaders are charismatic in that they have a vision about the future and instil others with the excitement to follow and help realise the vision (Conger, 1991). This approach to exceptional leadership is not a return to the 'great person' theory we considered earlier (section 5.3) but is seen as the effect and reactions that charismatic or transformational leaders have on their followers. Conger (1991) identifies four main characteristics of leader–follower relationships as follows:

1   Followers show high levels of devotion, loyalty and reverence to the leader.
2   Followers are both enthusiastic and committed to the ideas and vision espoused by the leader.
3   Followers willingly make self-sacrifices for the general good of the group as a whole.
4   Followers show levels of performance and behaviour greatly beyond what would normally be expected.

This paints a picture of followers as devoted to the leader whom they hold almost in awe and reverence. Many cult leaders can be seen in this way as well as highly influential figures such as Adolf Hitler and Lenin.

Howell and Frost (1989) have analysed the key behaviours that transformational leaders show when having such a profound influence on their followers. First, a vision or dream which the leader is able to communicate in vivid, exciting and emotional ways. Second, such leaders convince their followers that they have a path or means to get them from where they are now to a realisation of the dream. Third, they offer framing (Conger, 1991) in which their movement or organisation offers justification and reason for getting followers to behave in ways they want them to behave. Transformational leaders also exhibit total confidence in what they say and do, deep regard for the needs of their followers, excellent interpersonal communication skills and an enthralling, inspirational power of oration (House *et al.*, 1991). Palich and Hom (1992) have shown that workers who have total confidence in their leader and see him or her as highly competent both perform at higher levels and allow their leader to lead.

House *et al.* (1991) conducted archival research to investigate charisma among 31 previous American presidents. They found, as predicted, that highly charismatic presidents evinced strong needs for power and used this power to obtain social rather than personal goals. Their research also gave some insight into the circumstances under which charismatic leaders are most likely to emerge. These are when the leader is deeply involved and expects high levels of commitment from followers, and in times of crisis or instability.

Interest in transformational or charismatic leadership has been intense in the 1990s because of the dramatic change and influence one person can bring about. Transformational leadership is a two-edged sword, however, since both good and bad may result. Such a leader may act to make people's lives better and create beneficial social change, or act for selfish, immoral reasons and create social division and personal unhappiness. To predict whether such a leader will have a positive or negative effect requires not only an understanding of the situation but also a deeper psychological analysis about the motives and principles according to which the person is behaving. To date, this deeper research into the psyche of such leaders has yet to be conducted.

Gender and culture

Female leaders

Our examination of leadership to this point has not considered differences that may or may not exist between men and women as leaders, or whether there are cultural differences in leadership style. We will consider each in turn in this section.

The examples of well-known leaders given at the start of this chapter and in the preceding section were predominantly male. In asking you to think about leaders you have heard about, it is most likely that your list was also mostly male. This raises the question of whether or not males and females differ in leadership style or leadership effectiveness in such a way as to prevent women from occupying top positions. Another explanation may be that cultural stereotypes of women prevent them from attaining top leadership positions, especially when most of those are usually held by men in the first place. Social psychologists have conducted extensive research into these issues.

Eagly and Johnson (1990) conducted a meta-analytic review of over 150 studies of leadership to see if males and females differ in their leadership styles. They considered such dimensions as task-oriented vs. socio-emotional, and autocratic vs. democratic leadership styles. The most important overall finding was that male and female leaders show similar approaches to performing tasks and maintaining interpersonal relationships. However, this review also showed some difference between male and female leaders in work settings: males were generally more directive and autocratic, while females were more democratic and participative in their leadership styles. Earlier research had shown that women who use a more directive, autocratic style of leadership are generally perceived in a negative light by their workers (Denmark, 1980). A negative effect for women who hold traditionally male leadership positions also seems to occur – such women are seen as less feminine and more masculine in terms of personality characteristics (Eagly *et al.*, 1992). It was also found that men evaluated female leaders occupying traditionally male positions more negatively than did females.

Sex discrimination is rightly frowned on in this country and laws exist to help stop such discrimination. However, while people may not communicate or talk about the real attitudes they hold, negative views of women as leaders may be revealed in other ways, especially through non-verbal behaviours. Butler and Geis (1990) observed the facial expressions of a male and female confederate working with two other naïve participants in four-person groups. The researchers staged matters such that the confederates assumed leadership positions at different times over the period that the group worked together. When the confederates took a leadership position, observers behind a two-way mirror recorded the number of smiles and frowns shown by the naïve participants. As may be seen from Figure 6.6, more smiles were displayed when a man took the leadership position and more frowns when the female took leadership.

Discrimination and bias against women as leaders may be quite subtle, but may also be picked up on by female leaders and act as a deterrent or reduce their self-confidence.

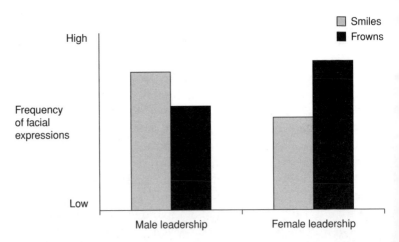

FIGURE 6.6 Frequency of smiles and frowns shown by participants to males and females assuming a leadership position in a small group

Source: adapted from Butler and Geis (1990)

In relation to leadership effectiveness it seems that men are more effective in positions seen as traditionally male, and women are more effective in positions seen as traditionally female (Eagly *et al.*, 1995). In concrete terms this has been described as interpersonal abilities, co-operativeness and getting along with workers for women, and directiveness and control of others for men. Men have also been seen to be more effective in male-dominated organisations and where most followers are also men.

Research clearly supports the claim that women experience a 'glass ceiling', and that when they break through the glass they are viewed more positively and are likely to be more effective by maintaining a leadership that is participative and democratic. However, this may be due to the negative reactions of men to women operating a more 'masculine' style of leadership. Finally, female transformational leaders show the same behavioural style and approach to their followers as do males. Exceptional leadership transcends the sex of the leader.

Cultural differences

Hofstede (1980) conducted a classic and influential large-scale cross-cultural study of work-related values which has been used to compare different cultures on a range of psychological characteristics. The two important dimensions for comparing leadership style and effectiveness across cultures have been:

1 *Power distance*   – high when employees or followers are afraid to express disagreement with their managers or leaders. Low when not afraid.

2 *Individualism vs. collectivism*   – collectivistic cultures show greater concern for the welfare of other people, while individualistic cultures emphasise personal identity and individual freedom.

Hofstede found that collectivist cultures, such as China, tended to be high on power distance, while individualistic cultures, such as the USA and Great Britain, were low on power distance. How then might this relate to leadership?

Fiedler's contingency theory of leadership distinguishes between task-oriented and socio-emotional styles of leadership. It seems, however, that this may be a reflection of western, individualistic cultures (Yukl, 1994). Misumi (1985) conducted a large number of studies in Japan, a more collectivist culture, in a range of different companies (government offices, shipyards, bus companies and banks) and found that the most effective leaders are those who score high on *both* task-oriented and socio-emotional measures of leadership. Misumi did conceptualise these two styles slightly differently to Fiedler, calling them 'performance' and 'maintenance' behaviours. Bond and Hwang (1986) conducted a review of leadership studies in Taiwan and provided further support for the idea that effective leaders combined both styles to a high level.

Leadership effectiveness may also be a function of the type of challenges faced by leaders. This was investigated by Peterson *et al.* (1995) using senior managers across 22 nations. Using a measure of distance power, these researchers found that work overload was characteristic of managers of high power distance cultures, and role ambiguity characteristic of low power distance cultures. This means that in high distance power cultures effective managers will be able to prioritise tasks well, while in low distance power cultures managers will be making decisions on the basis of less than complete information.

Research in the above areas has largely produced evidence for leadership differences between cultures; however, the transformational leader seems to be universal across cultures (Bass and Avolio, 1993). Using a questionnaire designed to measure the extent to which a leader is transformational, Bass and Avolio (1993) found commonality in such leaders across a range of countries including the USA, Japan, Spain, Germany and India. Visionary leaders, therefore, seem to have the same relationship and effect on followers regardless of culture and, by inference, across different time periods. This means a transformational leader is likely to be as influential now as a thousand years ago or a thousand years into the future. Clearly there is something fundamental that such a leader taps into in human beings.

Overview

In this chapter we have looked at a wide range of theories of leadership. What conclusion, if any, may be drawn? First, there is no one simple explanation of leadership: personality, behavioural style, the situation and the goals of the leader all have a role to play in helping us understand what makes an effective leader. Second, while much of the emphasis has been on leadership effectiveness, it is of value to look at the rise and fall, success and failure, of leaders. For example, Margaret Thatcher was Prime Minister for 11 years and successfully led the Conservative Party in three general elections. At the end her fall as leader was swift and dramatic. How is this to be explained in relation to the theories we have considered? Perhaps her autocratic style eventually caused such discontent among her male ministers that they lost confidence in her as a leader. Perhaps her more stereotypically masculine approach to the role lost favour among male and female party members alike. You may speculate on other explanations yourself.

Finally, the more recent interest in exceptional leaders by way of transformational or charismatic leadership is of value because such people are highly influential and may cause dramatic change. However, only a few people in leadership positions are of this calibre. Given this, psychologists need also to maintain theoretical and research interests in the more 'mundane' aspects of leadership.

Summary

Leadership may be regarded as social influence; influence may be achieved through the use of one or more type of power – reward, referent, informational, legitimate, expert and coercive power.

Attempts to identify personality traits specific to great leaders has generally failed; at best only weak evidence exists for traits of intelligence, extraversion, dominance and sensitivity to others. Two types of behavioural style seem to characterise leaders: directive behaviours and consideration behaviours. These are similar to those of task-oriented and socio-emotional found by Bales. Lippett and White (1943) investigated the effects of autocratic, democratic and *laissez-faire* leadership styles and found that the democratic style produced both good levels of performance and high individual satisfaction. Fiedler's contingency theory of leadership states that the behavioural style – task-oriented or socio-emotional – and situational favourableness are needed to predict when a leader will be effective. The normative theory of leadership suggests that three decision-making styles – autocratic, consultative, and participative – need to be considered in relation to two situational factors – need for high-quality decision and follower acceptance – to predict effectiveness.

Path–goal theory characterises leadership as providing a means or path by which a goal may be attained. Four leadership styles are suggested: directive, supportive, participative, achievement-oriented. Transformational or charismatic leaders are visionaries who develop a special relationship with their followers. Such leaders may act to the good or detriment of society or humanity. Sex of the leader and cultural differences have been found to affect leadership style and effectiveness. Similarities between male and female leaders outweigh differences; however, stereotypes may have negative effects for female leaders.

Further reading

Bass, B. M. (1990) *Bass and Stogdill's Handbook of Leadership* (3rd edn), New York: Free Press. A full and comprehensive treatment of theory and research on leadership over the past 50 years. A book to dip into. A little dated but still the best sustained treatment of leadership.

Bass, B. M. (1997) Does the transactional-transformational leadership paradigm transcend organisational and national boundaries?,

American Psychologist, 52 (2), 130–139. A highly readable short article outlining the basics of transformational leadership and reviewing evidence about its potential universality.

Senge, P. M. (199) *The Fifth Discipline: The Art and Practice of the Learning Organization*, New York: Doubleday. A highly regarded and influential approach to leadership in applied, organisational settings. A best-seller and popular text in organisational psychology – also accessible to read.

Simonton, D. K. (1994) *Greatness: Who Makes History and Why?*, New York: Guilford Press. This book deals with great leaders and provides an analysis in terms of transformational leadership.

Chapter 7

Individual and group decision-making

Introduction

I MAGINE THE POST ARRIVES one morning and among the letters is an official-looking one; you open it and read that you have been selected for jury service. Four weeks later you find yourself in court after having listened to a case where the prosecution alleged burglary. The jury, of which you are a member, has just retired to consider making a verdict. You are with 11 other people whom you have not met before. The jury has to make an important decision that may have a profound affect upon a person's life. You have to make up your own mind and make an individual decision; the jury has to make a collective decision which should also be unanimous.

The jury as a decision-making group is perhaps one of the most researched areas in applied social psychology (Pennington and Hastie, 1990). From the perspective of individual and group decision-making it is easy to see why: consideration of jury decision-making touches on whether a rational or more intuitive approach is made, how an individual's decision is influenced and reached, and what group phenomena may take place to influence and potentially bias the final outcome of the jury's deliberations. These are all topics that we consider in some detail in this chapter. As you read through, you may wish to consider how the topic or issue under consideration may apply to a jury.

A note of caution is needed however. A jury is an unusual decision-making group mainly because it brings together a disparate group of people on just one occasion to make decisions. A jury is unlike work groups which may have been together for some time and selected members for the experience and expertise they offer. In Chapter 1 we considered a wide range of different types of groups; what follows applies to these also. The use of a jury to open this chapter was chosen to help 'bring to life' some of the theories and concepts we discuss below.

Approaches to decision-making

In broad terms we may characterise individual decision-making as either rational or intuitive; the former reflects a logical, ordered and thought-through approach; the latter relates to 'gut feelings' and insights a person may have about what decision to reach. In many ways we probably like to think of ourselves as rational decision-makers; in reality decision-making is most likely to result from a mix of both approaches (Greenberg and Baron, 1993).

Rational decision-making

The rational approach to decision-making (Harrison, 1995) has traditionally broken down the process into six separate steps. These are summarised in Figure 7.1. Not all decisions will be analysable into these six separate stages; some steps may need to be combined or left out, depending on the nature of the problem facing the decision-maker.

The first step is *problem identification* which includes recognition both that a problem or decision is required, and that some action has to be taken. While this may seem straightforward, considerable evidence exists to show that people often ignore, misperceive or imagine that a problem does not exist in the first place (Cowan, 1986). This may happen especially when a very unpleasant and painful decision has to be made. For example, ending a long-standing relationship or having to decide to make workers redundant because the future of a company is not good (in the latter case an executive may not recognise that the company's future is poor). Clear, accurate and realistic identification of a problem is the first step in the decision-making process.

The second step is the *diagnostic phase* which includes considerations such as the urgency of the problem, how much or

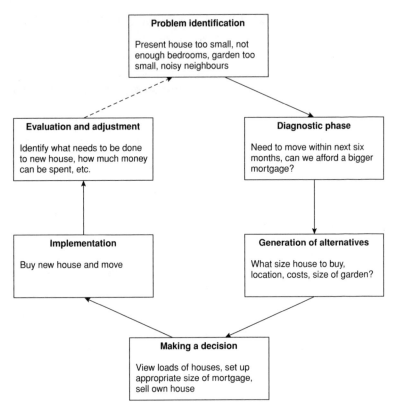

FIGURE 7.1 Six-step model of rational decision-making highlighted through the example of deciding to move house

how little it may be shared by others and what information exists to identify the nature of the problem. The diagnostic phase should also include an assessment of whether the problem can be solved or a decision reached. This may be done in relation to the time-scales and information needed to make a properly considered decision.

The next step is the *generation of alternatives* in which possible solutions to the problem are identified. This may make use of such techniques as brainstorming, the nominal group technique and the Delphi technique (see Chapter 3, section 3.5). One of the dangers during this phase is that alternatives may be evaluated and rejected prematurely and a decision selected from an impoverished range of alternatives.

The fourth stage is *making a decision* in which the alternatives should be evaluated in light of the information available and the outcome that the person or group is seeking to achieve. Careful exploration of consequences of a decision, both intended and unintended, is required at this stage to ensure undesirable consequences do not outweigh the desirable consequences of a decision.

The next step is the *implementation* of the decision, where the decision is taken and the individual or group involved accepts that they are accountable and responsible for the decision. If this does not happen, negative effects on the final phase of *evaluation and adjustment* may ensue. In this final phase the effectiveness, consequences and changes that taking and implementing the decision has brought about need to be monitored. Implementing a decision very rarely results in the desired outcome being achieved fully, and unintended consequences may also result. This leads back to the first step of identifying what the problems of the decision have produced as a result.

As can be seen from this six-step approach, rational decision-making is a cyclical process and requires the individual or group to be constantly vigilant and aware of what is going on at each step. This model makes certain assumptions which may not always be met and may thus question its applicability. First it is assumed that the problem is clear and unambiguous and that a high level of information is available or can be found to help inform the decision. Second, it is assumed that all viable decision alternatives can be identified and the consequences of each possible decision determined. Third, the different decisions that could be made can be ranked and evaluated in such a way as to identify the optimum decision. Fourth and finally, that time to take a decision and obtaining sufficient information to allow a decision to be made are not constraining factors. No doubt there are more assumptions you can think of; the general message is that while such an approach may be highly desirable, it is unlikely that all the underlying assumptions can be met in any real-life setting. This may compromise the rational approach and has led some researchers to look more seriously at the intuitive approach to decision-making.

Intuitive decision-making

While a logical, orderly and well-informed approach to decision-making may be highly desirable, since it allows other people to see how a decision was reached, there are elements which tap our powers of creativity more than the ability to think logically. Creative solutions to problems are often superior to those arrived at in a logical way, and, in a world of increasingly rapid change, creativity is just as important as logical thought. Choosing a decision alternative often reflects an individual's (or group's) personal values, ethical standards and subjective views. In addition, facing the same problem or situation may result in different people making different decisions as a reflection of the personal aspects mentioned above. This has been recognised over the past decade (Mitchell and Beach, 1990) and one model built on an intuitive approach is that of *image theory* (Mitchell and Beach, 1990).

The rational approach is time-consuming and quite complex; by contrast, image theory is fast and simple because it is claimed that people make decisions intuitively with a minimal amount of cognitive effort. This reflects sayings such as 'it seems the right thing to do' or 'I'm not sure this is the right thing for us whatever the merits'. More formally, image theory presents a simple two-stage model based on a *compatibility test* and a *profitability test*. For the compatibility test questions are put such as: Is this decision or course of action consistent with our values, goals and plans we have for the future? If the answer is 'no' the decision alternative is rejected outright; if the answer is 'yes' the second stage comes into play. This is the profitability test which looks at a range of alternatives to see which one fits best with values, goals and future plans. The one that fits best is then selected. The image model relies on underlying rationality since in a company setting, for example, there must be a clear statement of the values, goals and future plans of the company that is both understood

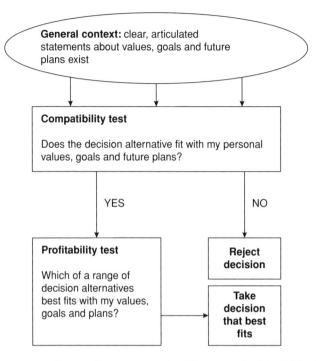

FIGURE 7.2 Image theory as an intuitive model of individual or group decision-making

Source: adapted from Mitchell and Beach (1990)

and committed to by its employees, particularly those at a senior level with important decision-making responsibilities.

Figure 7.2 depicts this model. Try to apply it to yourself in relation to, for example, deciding whether or not to take a job working in a chicken processing factory or agreeing to promote genetically modified foods.

Given the combination of intuition and logic that is embedded in this model it is fair to claim that it is not a purely intuitive model, but relies on a combination of intuition (creativity, insight, unusual solutions) and rationality (clear statement and articulation of values, goals and plans). One factor which heavily impacts on the implementation of decisions made on a more intuitive basis is an assessment of the riskiness of a decision. This is accounted for in the rational model through the evaluation of alternatives under-taken before a decision is made. With intuitive approaches risk may be assessed by both objective and subjective means to arrive at an assessment of whether a decision is high or low in its level of risk. High-risk decisions may be dangerous but bring with them great rewards if successful.

Most decision-making takes place under conditions of uncer-tainty in terms of obtaining the planned for and desired outcome. At times the level of uncertainty may be assessed and at other times people may be subject to certain biases or judgemental errors when attempting to make such assessments. We will look at these issues from the perspective of the individual decision-maker.

Individual decision-making

People differ in the approach they take to decision-making and a number of different ways of conceptualising individual differences have been made. Here we shall look at decision-making styles and the rational-economic and administrative models. The section will conclude by considering the errors and biases to which individuals are typically subject when making decisions.

Decision-making styles

Rowe *et al.* (1984) conceptualised individual decision-making along two separate dimensions: ways of thinking and tolerance for ambiguity. Reflecting the rational and intuitive approaches we have considered previously in this chapter, the ways of thinking dimen-sion is categorised as either rational or intuitive. The second dimension recognises that different people differ in the extent to which they are able to tolerate ambiguity. Some people require decision situations to be highly structured with well-organised and good levels of information. Other people are able to oper-ate well in the relative absence of such features. This yields a high–low tolerance for ambiguity dichotomy. Characterising each dimension in two ways yields, according to Rowe *et al.* (1984),

TABLE 7.1   Individual decision-making styles suggested by Rowe *et al.* (1984)

Analytic style	*Conceptual style*
Rational and high tolerance for ambiguity	Intuitive and high tolerance for ambiguity
Careful decision-maker, adaptable and flexible	Interested in long-term plans or vision. Creative solutions forthcoming

Directive style	*Behavioural style*
Rational and low tolerance for ambiguity	Intuitive and low tolerance for ambiguity
Logical and efficient at making decisions, but may consider only small number of alternatives	Works well with others and good communicator

four individual decision-making styles: directive, analytic, conceptual and behavioural. These are depicted in Table 7.1.

The *directive style* occurs where there is a low tolerance for ambiguity and a rational approach – such people may be seen as logical and efficient, making decisions fast but often only assessing a small number of alternatives. Such a decision-making style will not fare well in situations of high ambiguity where little information is readily available. The *analytic style* has a high tolerance for ambiguity – such people are characterised as careful decision-makers who usually request a considerable amount of further information. They are regarded as adaptable and flexible but may not work well with intuitive decision-makers. A *conceptual style* of decision-making tends to have more interest in longer term plans for an organisation and may be good at suggesting creative solutions and ideas to problems. Finally, the *behavioural style* is characterised by people who work well with others and have a regard for the well-being of those they are working with. This style also exhibits conflict avoidance and communicates well with other people. If you have already read Chapter 6 on leadership, you may think the directive and behavioural decision-making styles are similar to the task-oriented or autocratic leader and socio-emotional leader respectively. This is probably the case; however, the approach here has value because it applies to all decision-making, and not just to that by leaders or senior executives in an organisation. The model by Rowe *et al.* (1984) has enjoyed considerable appeal to management training but has lacked a substantial empirical base of evidence. Nevertheless, it does help to identify how individuals differ in their decision-making styles and suggests how people might change better to fit the environment in which they work.

Rational-economic and administrative models

Models of decision-making may be broadly classified into one of two types. First, *normative* models which prescribe or provide rules and guidelines about how one should approach and make a decision. Normative models present an ideal which people then try their best to achieve. Second, *descriptive* models which attempt to characterise how decision-makers actually go about the task of decision-making. Descriptive models are not based on an ideal but represent what actually takes place in practice. Here we look at an example of each of these types of models: the rational-economic which is normative and the administrative which is descriptive (Simon, 1979).

The rational-economic model is really an idealised form of the analytic style of decision-making which we looked at in the previous section. This model requires the decision-maker to identify all possible alternative courses of action that are open to him or her, and then fully to assess the viability of each based on complete information. The outcome for this model is that the optimal or very best decision is made. This model assumes that decision-makers are perfectly rational and logical, and are able to integrate and use all available information (Simon, 1979). While it represents an attractive ideal to which decision-makers should be encouraged to aspire, using such a model is not only time-consuming and slow, but places huge demands on the cognitive processes of the individual; they go way beyond what any individual may actually be capable of.

It is well recognised that individuals have limited information-processing capabilities, making it difficult if not impossible to assimilate and understand all the information which is potentially available. Information technology in the form of specialised software packages has helped. However, ultimately it is the person who has to put the picture together who arrives at a decision. In addition, it may be that the rational-economic model is not the best way to solve problems. Frederickson and Mitchell (1984) conducted research on the decision-making of senior managers and found that the more comprehensive an organisation's approach to decision-making, the less well the company performed financially. Minimalist approaches were also linked to poor performance. The message then is that a balance needs to be struck between ideal and practical considerations. The *administrative model* offers this, since it characterises decision-makers as limited processors of information when considering only a limited range of alternatives (March and Simon, 1958; Simon, 1957). Two key ideas are used in this model: bounded rationality and satisficing. *Bounded rationality* occurs where simplified characterisations of the situation are made which represent the essential information without the level of complexity that really exists. Having constructed a simplified view of reality the decision-maker is then said to behave in a rational way (Simon, 1976). The concept of *satisficing* represents the idea that decision-makers select an alternative that is good enough for a given situation, often recognising that the decision taken is not the optimal one. A decision that satisfices is satisfactory and likely to be acceptable to all those involved. We will see in the next section (section 7.3.3) how people use a range of 'cognitive short-cuts' or heuristics of thinking to allow them to process potentially large amounts of information in making a judgement.

The two models may be compared in relation to a number of criteria. For example, in the rational-economic model the

TABLE 7.2 Differences between the rational-economic and administrative models of decision-making

Assumption	Rational-economic model	Administrative model
Degree of rationality	Perfect rationality	Bounded rationality
Information	Complete processing	Limited processing
Decision alternative	Optional choice	Satisficing choice
Type of model	Normative	Descriptive

Source: adapted from Greenberg and Baron (1993)

decision-maker is depicted as perfectly rational, while the administrative model depicts the decision-maker as operating according to bounded rationalities. Table 7.2 summarises some of the key differences between the models.

You may wonder why psychologists produce normative or prescriptive models of decision-making when it seems more valuable accurately to describe how decision-making actually takes place. One reason is that an ideal is needed as a bench-mark so that differences between ideal and actual may be determined. Another, related reason is that when poor decisions are taken an analysis can be conducted to identify what went wrong and adjustments made so that the same error or mistake is not repeated in the future. Finally, descriptive models themselves represent a level of abstraction in order to characterise the decision-making process; however, a descriptive model is based on observation while a normative model is based on principles and ideals that may not be primarily derived from observation. From this analysis you will appreciate that there is usually a constant interplay between the two models which is needed for decision-makers to learn and improve as they become more experienced.

Heuristics of thinking

We have seen with the rational-economic and administrative models of decision-making that detailed information together with a high level of cognitive effort is required. In everyday life, and in many work groups where time pressures and deadlines impose constraints, people are not able to devote time and effort to a decision. In such circumstances an individual may fall back on past experience, social norms and intuitive approaches. One such approach has been called *heuristics of thinking* (Tversky and Kahneman, 1973); these occur when mental short-cuts or simple rules of thumb are used to arrive at a decision quickly and with little effort. Three of the most widely accepted and researched are the heuristics of *availability*, *representativeness*, and *anchoring and adjustment*.

Availability heuristic

The availability heuristic is exemplified when a person's judgement is influenced by the ease with which he or she can bring relevant instances or information to mind (Tversky and Kahneman, 1982). For example, the reporting in the press of tragic air accidents where large numbers of people have died may lead us to think flying is unsafe and high risk (whereas in reality aeroplanes and trains are safer than cars). In a different context, imagine you are trying to assess the risk of adopting a new computer system for your company. This may be influenced by recent media articles on how easily 'computer hackers' can cause huge damage to the system. Such examples of hacking may be readily available in your thinking and may be unduly influential. As another example, look back to the start of this chapter – the jury and burglary case. Imagine you are a juror and you are looking at the defendant across the court. He has a shaved head, tattoos on his arms, and earrings and a nose ring. This individual may bring to mind or make available other examples of people dressed in this way whom you have seen on television and who are criminals.

The availability heuristic, then, does not require a lot of mental effort and time on the part of the individual but may reflect a biased set of examples and so lead to poor judgements or faulty decision-making. In a group setting or decision-making group the biasing or negative effect of the availability heuristic may be less in evidence. This may be the case since five or six individuals may bring different instances to mind, thus cancelling out the bias of any one individual. Of course, if we all bring the same instances to mind, which may be culturally determined, bias may be even stronger.

Rothman and Hardin (1997) showed, through a series of experiments, that the availability heuristic may have two components. These are, first, the ease with which relevant information or examples come to mind (the traditional view of the availability heuristic) and, second, the sheer amount of information that comes to mind. Rothman and Hardin (1997) went on to show that judgements based on facts and information are more likely to use the amount of information version of availability. In contrast, judgements involving emotions or feelings rely more on the ease of information version of availability.

The availability heuristic, then, is a simple heuristic or cognitive device for making judgements or decisions. However, it may lead to error or bias because of the idiosyncratic nature of what any one individual brings to mind.

Representativeness heuristic

The representativeness heuristic is the rule that 'the more similar an individual is to typical members of a given group, the more likely he or she is to belong to that group' (Baron and Byrne, 2000, p.86). This heuristic applies equally well to events and objects as to people. Tversky and Kahneman (1973) provided the following description of a person:

> Steve is very shy and withdrawn, invariably helpful, but with little interest in people or reality. A meek and tidy soul, he has a need for order and structure and a passion for detail.

Participants in an experiment were all given this description of Steve; however, half were told that this description was randomly selected from 100 where 30 per cent were librarians and 70 per cent were engineers. The other half of the participants were told that the decision was taken from a sample where 30 per cent were engineers and 70 per cent were librarians. In the former case, relative to the respective baselines, participants greatly over-estimated the chances of the above description being that of a librarian. The description is highly representative of the common stereotype or typical librarian to such an extent that participants ignore or take very little account of the sample distribution or, as it is more commonly called, *base rates*.

Hence, the rule of thumb for judging how representative the individual is of a category or social group may lead to error or bias because base rates are ignored. However, base rate information is not always ignored, especially when it has high personal relevance to yourself and is easily understandable. For example, suppose you are deciding which option module to select on your course of study. One module appeals to your own interests, but you find out that the failure rate on this module was 40 per cent last year. You look at another module which is less interesting to you personally, but the failure rate last year was only 5 per cent. Which module do you think you would be likely to select?

The representativeness heuristic is a useful mental short-cut to aid decision-making, and is likely to be of greater use if base rate information can be made relevant and of personal importance to the individual.

Anchoring and adjustment heuristic

The anchoring and adjustment heuristic occurs when an individual starts from an initial position or anchor and makes an adjustment in the light of subsequent information provided. Typically, research shows that people do not adjust enough and remain too strongly influenced by the initial anchor point (Tversky and Kahneman, 1973). For example, Greenberg *et al.* (1980) conducted a mock jury study whereby half the participants or mock jurors were asked to consider the harshest verdict first. The other half were asked to consider the most lenient verdict first. With the former instruction, jurors returned a relatively harsh verdict compared with jurors given the latter, lenient instruction.

Expectations may often act as an anchor. For example, Cervone and Peake (1986) asked students to guess how many out of 20 anagrams they thought they could correctly solve. Before asking the students to give an estimate, half were asked 'will you get more than four correct?' and the other half 'will you get fewer than 18 correct?' Those given the anchor of four estimated they would solve fewer anagrams than those given the anchor of 18. Generally, then, how you give estimates and make judgements about the likelihood of success may be unduly influenced by the anchor, starting point or initial expectation that you have.

The three heuristics of thinking we have looked at here – availability, representativeness, and anchoring and adjustment – all offer mental short-cuts to judgements and decision-making. However, caution is needed when using them since error and bias may result.

Group decision-making

Many of the decisions that are made in such settings as work, government, the criminal system are based on a small group of people coming to an agreement over a decision. For example, the jury with a verdict of guilty or innocent with respect to a particular charge; the board of directors of a company with respect to whether to take over another company; the government Cabinet with respect to an environmental policy. These groups are generally relatively small in size, often no more than 20 people, and sometimes much smaller. Social psychologists have paid considerable attention to group decision-making processes and outcomes. Here we shall look at *social decision schemes* and *group polarisation*.

Social decision schemes

Perhaps the most commonly regarded approach to group decision-making is that of *consensus*. However, 'consensus decision-making' is a term that is used as a catch-all for trying to reach a judgement or decision by mutual agreement within the group. The problem with this type of definition is that it is too broad and generally applicable to be of much value. Social psychologists (Napier and Gershenfeld, 1999) specify more precisely the conditions that must exist for consensus decision-making. These are detailed in Table 7.3.

TABLE 7.3 The five factors of trust, awareness, leadership, time and information required for consensus decision-making

Factor	Description
Trust	A high level of trust should exist between group members – this permits honesty, directness and candour
Awareness	Members of the group are aware of the processes and are able to deal with unhelpful behaviour, such as dominance or manipulativeness, of individuals
Leadership	The leader does not dominate the group but directs, summarises and facilitates
Time	Time is available to consider options, different views, potential consequences of actions taken, etc.
Information	All members of the group have access to and are familiar with all the information available

As you can see, these are stringent requirements which many decision-making groups would have to work hard to live up to and would need to be allowed adequate time to meet together as a group. The benefits of groups operating a proper consensual approach to decision-making are high levels of group satisfaction, strong commitment to the decision reached and effective decision-making (Schweiger *et al.*, 1986). The price for consensual decision-making is time, training, a willingness to resolve conflict, and letting go of personal agendas for the good of the group as a whole and the decision reached. In many types of real-life and organisation settings this price is often too high, and more pragmatic approaches to decision-making are adopted.

Social decision schemes (Davis, 1973; Strasser *et al.*, 1989) offer a small number of simple rules that have been shown to be reasonably accurate in predicting the final decision of a group from knowledge of each group member's position or view. These are summarised in Table 7.4. Research has shown that these five simple rules are accurate about 80 per cent of the time (Strasser

TABLE 7.4 Identification and description of the five social decision schemes suggested by Davis (1973) and Strasser *et al.* (1989)

Social decision scheme	Description
Unanimity	All group members are required to agree on the decision reached
Majority wins	Group decision will be determined by the option that has the support of a simple majority in the group
Truth wins	Group will select the correct decision or judgement, even if not supported by all group members
Two-thirds majority	Decision reached will be that supported by at least two-thirds of the group members
First shift	Decision reached will reflect the first shift in opinion or change of mind shown by any member of the group

et al., 1989). Different types of tasks set for the group tend to determine the type of social decision scheme or rule adopted. For example, problem-solving tasks where there is only one correct answer generally result in the group using the truth wins rule. By contrast, tasks which are more judgemental and do not have an obvious correct answer, which are most common in organisational settings, result in the group adopting a majority wins rule (Laughlin and Ellis, 1986).

These five social decision schemes may be categorised along a dimension of *power concentration*. At one end of the spectrum would be high power concentration (power concentrated on one or a few group members) and at the other end of the spectrum would be low power concentration (power distributed among all group members). For example, unanimity has low power concentration, and two-thirds majority, higher power concentration. The social decision scheme of unanimity is the one most similar to consensus, as defined earlier. As such, research has shown that group satisfaction with the decision reached, satisfaction with the group decision and positive feelings between group members is higher with the unanimity rule (Miller, 1989).

A word of caution is needed, however, since these five social decision schemes characterise well the actual practice of decision, but may not always result in good decisions. For example, Strasser (1992) has shown that group members tend to spend more time discussing information known to all group members rather than information known to only a minority of group members. Failure to share and discuss information known only to a few group members may be to the overall detriment of the group. This is something we shall take up when we look at groupthink later in this chapter.

Group polarisation

Imagine you are a member of a group in an organisation that has been asked to decide how best to invest money in stocks and shares. Two key options present themselves: you can either invest in shares that are safe and will yield a modest return for the company, or you can make a high-risk investment which may yield high returns. The group discusses the options, individuals express their opinions, and a decision is about to be reached. Will the group go for the risky option or the safe bet?

Early research by Stoner (1961) suggested that even where groups followed a good decision-making process of discussion and looking at different options, the group decision was riskier than that of individuals in the group. This tendency was called the *risky shift*, and, perhaps not surprisingly, captured the attention of social psychologists and organisational psychologists alike.

In what follows we first look at research on the risky shift and identify when it may or may not apply. We then move on to consider the idea of *group polarisation* which may be defined as 'the tendency of group members, as a result of group discussion, to shift towards more extreme positions than those originally held' (Baron and Byrne, 2001, p. 86). The risky shift became subsumed into the more general phenomenon of group polarisation.

Risky shift

The risky shift was based on the use of *choice* dilemmas (Kogan and Wallach, 1964). In each choice dilemma you would be asked to read about an imaginary dilemma facing a person and then advise on the degree of risk you think the person should take. One of Kogan and Wallach's (1964) dilemmas runs as follows:

> Mr A, an electrical engineer, who is married and has one child, has been working for a large electronics corporation since graduating from university five years ago. He is assured of a lifetime job with a modest, although adequate, salary and liberal pension benefits upon retirement. On the other hand, it is very unlikely that his salary will increase greatly. While attending a conference, Mr A is offered a job with a small, newly formed company which has a highly uncertain future. The new job would pay more to start and would offer a share of the ownership if the company survived the competition of the larger firms.
>
> Imagine that you are advising Mr A. Listed below are several probabilities or odds of the new company being financially sound. Please indicate the lowest probability that you would consider acceptable to make it worthwhile for Mr A to take the new job.

- The chances are one in ten that the company will prove financially sound.
- The chances are three in ten that the company will prove financially sound.
- The chances are five in ten that the company will prove financially sound.
- The chances are seven in ten that the company will prove financially sound.
- The chances are nine in ten that the company will prove financially sound.

- Mr A should not take the new job no matter what the probabilities.

Participants were first asked, on an individual basis and before being allocated to a group, to indicate what advice they would give Mr A as regards the *lowest* acceptable probability that would justify taking up the new position. Participants were then put into groups of six and discussed the dilemma until a unanimous decision (or majority decision, if this proved impossible) was reached. Finally, participants were then asked their individual opinion following group discussion. Kogan and Wallach (1964) found that, for this dilemma, the unanimous group view was riskier than the average opinions of the individuals before group discussion. In addition, individual views were riskier on average after group discussion. Numerous other studies provided support for the risky shift phenomenon (Cartwright, 1971; Dion *et al.*, 1970).

However, subsequent research reported a *cautious shift* – this is where group discussion results in a group decision that is more cautious or risk avoidant compared to average individual views before group discussion (Fraser *et al.*, 1971; Turner *et al.*, 1989). Typically cautious shifts are observed when matters have to do with personal health, for example.

The findings that some choice dilemmas produced risky shifts and others cautious shifts led psychologists to recognise a broader phenomenon called *group polarisation*.

Group polarisation

We have defined group polarisation as the tendency for group discussion to make individual views more extreme in the direction that such views were already taking. Hence an individual who initially advocates a risky option will, as a result of group discussion deciding a risky option, take a more risky position. The same would happen for someone starting off with a cautious opinion with the group discussion resulting in a cautious decision. In short, group polarisation occurs where the group decision is more extreme than, but in the same direction as, the initial position of the group members.

Group polarisation as a shift of individual views to more extreme positions may be applied more widely than just to cautious or risky type dilemma situations. It may be applied to situations where individuals may show opposition or favour to a certain decision. For example, people opposed to or in favour of capital punishment would be predicted to strengthen their initial view as a result of group discussion where the group as a whole tends towards the corresponding extreme. As another example, think back to the jury scenario given at the beginning of this chapter. If the individual views of jury members before discussion tend towards guilt, group discussion may result in the jury being even more harsh in its verdict.

Given that group polarisation is such a widespread phenomenon applicable in many different circumstances, what explanations have been offered? Three main explanations will be considered: social comparison, persuasive arguments and self-categorisation.

The *social comparison explanation* suggests that, depending on cultural norms, people often value opinions or views that are more extreme than their own. The result of engagement with group discussion is that individuals realise that their own position is not the norm and shift towards the prevailing and more extreme position shown by the other members of the group. Individuals may initially hold less extreme opinions or views for fear of being seen as deviant or extremist by others. The normative influence resulting from the knowledge of other people's views lifts this fear and allows the individual perhaps to share his or her more privately held opinion with others. Alternatively, individuals might adjust their views to that of others for reasons of social approval.

The *persuasive arguments explanation* (Burnstein, 1982) suggests that individuals are swayed by compelling arguments given by other group members in the discussion. Those who had originally adopted more moderate positions may be persuaded by arguments they were not aware of and shift position to the more extreme view. It has also been demonstrated that merely repeating one's own argument in favour of or against a position to other people strengthens the initially held opinion (Brauer et al., 1995).

Finally, the *self-categorisation explanation* (which could be seen as a variant of social comparison) of group polarisation states that people categorise themselves and identify with norms held by a group of which the person regards him- or herself to be a member. As long as the individual has a positive attitude to being a member of the group, the result will be to shift opinion to the more extremely held group norm (Turner and Oakes, 1989).

All three explanations of group polarisation offer valuable insight into why the phenomenon occurs. Evidence suggests that the social comparison explanation is more important than the persuasive arguments explanation (Zuber *et al.*, 1992).

Groupthink

Common sense has it that groups operate better than individuals and that group decision-making is likely to result in higher quality decisions than decisions made by individuals. This view has been strongly challenged by Janis (1982) who analysed a number of group decisions made at the highest level in the US government. As a result of such 'after-the-event' analyses, Janis (1982) suggested that defective group decision-making was a result of what he called *groupthink*. Janis (1982) claimed that groupthink occurs when members of a group seek concurrence, consensus and unanimity among themselves rather than critically looking at all options and deciding upon the best possible alternative. Groupthink is most likely to be evidenced in groups that are highly cohesive, and where time pressures and urgency to take decisions are high. Cohesion is one of the essential ingredients for a group to be able to work together (see Chapter 4). However, if cohesiveness in a group becomes extremely high, the individuals in the group will tend to do anything to maintain this. Highly cohesive groups are greatly valued by the individual group members – sometimes so much so that they become more concerned not to disrupt or threaten the group atmosphere. When the desire to maintain the enjoyment and high cohesiveness of the group takes priority over the reason the group has come together – to make important decisions –

TABLE 7.5 Symptoms or warning signals of groupthink

Warning signals	Description
Illusion of invulnerability	Over-optimistic, willing to take extreme risks, ignoring danger signals, feeling nothing can go wrong
Collective rationalisation	Discounting and discrediting information and signs that run counter to group thinking
Unquestioned morality	Belief that the group's thinking is ethical and moral, and that other views are evil
Excessive negative stereotyping	Seeing outsiders as negative and thinking their views are not valid
Strong conformity pressure	Dissent within the group is discouraged with penalties of disloyalty or expulsion
Self-censoring dissenting views	Individuals do not express alternative views or ideas to the rest of the group
Illusion of unanimity	False belief among all group members that everyone has same views, attitudes and judgement
Self-appointed mindguards	One person in the group takes on role of protecting group from negative, dissenting views and information

Source: adapted from Janis (1982)

groupthink is likely to occur. The warning signals or symptoms of groupthink are given in Table 7.5.

Notice what are really quite worrying warning signals; for example, one member of the group taking it upon him- or herself to act as what Janis calls a 'mindguard'. This person almost 'polices' the group to protect group members from different views, hide contradicting information and help ensure that the group believes in the consensus view that has been reached. Notice also that other symptoms include a feeling of invulnerability – that the collective wisdom of the group means it cannot make errors of judgement and be wrong. Further, that group members falsely believe that everybody else in the group agrees with what is said and the judgements made.

These symptoms of groupthink are seen to result in defective decision-making; the collective desire of the group to maintain high cohesiveness results in:

- an incomplete survey of alternative decisions or judgements that could be made;
- a failure properly to assess the risks of each of the decision options, particularly the decision reached;
- poor information search and a bias in how the limited amount of information obtained is processed;
- a failure to reconsider alternative decision options after having reached a decision;
- a failure to work through fully the potential consequences of a decision and hence make contingency plans.

Janis' (1982), and Janis and Mann's (1977) analysis of government policy-making groups has clarified the antecedent conditions, symptoms of groupthink and the defective decision-making that results. Further research by Janis (1989) has demonstrated that private sector business organisations are also susceptible to groupthink.

The methods used by Janis to produce evidence for groupthink have typically been based on *post hoc* or after-the-event analysis of defective policy decision-making. While this method has its values there may be a tendency for hindsight or being wise after the event to be present. That is, analysis of the antecedent conditions and symptoms of groupthink may be biased by knowledge of the outcome of a decision and the public condemnation of defective group decision-making.

Tetlock *et al.* (1992) attempted to provide a more objective approach to examining historical events. Here trained evaluators were asked to read about an event and provide ratings of the extent to which they felt the event showed evidence of the symptoms of groupthink. For example, one pair of statements used was as follows:

- The group leader is insulated from criticism

or

- The group leader is exposed to a wide range of views and arguments.

Tetlock *et al.* (1992) produced evidence for some aspects of groupthink (such as poor problem-solving procedures) but did not find that group cohesiveness on its own was central to the development of groupthink. Other research has criticised the groupthink idea because it has failed to take into account such factors as the power of the leader, the nature of the task facing the group, and the amount of time the group has existed with the same individual membership (Aldag and Fuller, 1993).

Some social psychological research has attempted to investigate groupthink through the use of traditional laboratory experiments. Turner *et al.* (1992) investigated groupthink by manipulating two key variables – representing important antecedent conditions identified by Janis. The two variables were group cohesiveness and stressful threat to the group. Participants allocated to high cohesiveness groups were given name tags and group identification to reinforce desirable group membership. Participants allocated to low cohesiveness groups did not receive name tags or group identity. Stressful threat to the group was either high or low; in the high-threat condition participants were told the group would be videotaped and the video used in training sessions. In the low-threat condition the participants were told the group discussion would remain confidential.

All groups were given an assembly production problem set in a car factory and asked to put forward a solution. The solutions were rated by the researchers on a five-point scale from low to high quality. As can be seen from Figure 7.3, high cohesive groups produced the lowest quality decision in the high-threat condition. By contrast, groups low in cohesiveness but in high threat produced

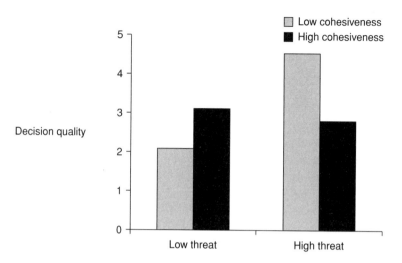

FIGURE 7.3 Decision quality by low and high cohesive groups in low- and high-threat conditions

Source: adapted from Turner *et al.* (1992)

the highest quality decision across the four experimental conditions. Notice also that high cohesive groups produced good-quality decisions in the low-threat condition.

From this experimental research we may conclude that poor decision-making does not necessarily follow as a result of high group cohesiveness. At least one other factor – threat to the group – is also needed, and where there is a low level of threat highly cohesive groups may in fact produce good-quality decisions.

Both this and other experimental research (Callaway *et al.*, 1985) together with the more structured historical approach of Tetlock *et al.* (1992) shows the concept of groupthink to be controversial, with mixed research evidence providing inconclusive support (Esser, 1998; Paulus, 1998). However, in certain circumstances groups do seem to make defective decisions which may be explained well by groupthink.

Preventing groupthink
One approach to helping groups avoid the pitfalls of groupthink is to look at the warning signals detailed in Table 7.5, and to

183

develop explicit instructions for groups to be aware and avoid their occurrence. Janis (1982) offers three pieces of advice. First, the leader of the group should facilitate each group member to express doubts and uncertainties, and to make this a regular overt strategy throughout group discussion. Second, the group leader should remain impartial and not let his or her views be known to the other group members. Third, the group should set up subgroups as well as referring their initial decisions to other independent groups. An additional strategy is to appoint somebody in the group to take on the role of 'devil's advocate'. This will help ensure that opinions, judgements and decisions are robustly challenged before the group agrees.

Rogelberg *et al.* (1992) have suggested a problem-solving strategy which they have called the *stepladder* approach. Here, a problem is initially given to a two-person group to discuss and explore solutions. After a while a third person joins the group and presents his or her views before the original two group members have to explain to the new person the discussion and solutions already considered. The new person challenges and questions the original two group members. Finally, after the three-person group has worked on the problem, a fourth person is introduced. The same process is then gone through. The overall idea behind this stepladder approach is that a fresh view is introduced at each of the two stages when a new person is introduced to the group. Rogelberg *et al.* (1992) found that group members felt less pressure to conform to the views of others in the group. Individuals also felt encouraged to add new ideas, opinions and solutions.

The above strategies that may be adopted to prevent or help reduce the likelihood of groupthink occurring have costs – mostly time and additional resources. Although these are scarce resources in the modern world they are needed to ensure important decisions that may affect many people's lives are of high quality and properly thought through.

Individuals or groups?

The question is often asked as to whether or not individuals or groups are better at making decisions. Not surprisingly the answer is 'it all depends'. On a simple task, the research shows that a group rarely performs better than the best individual in the group (Principle and Neeley, 1983). However, on more complex tasks requiring a range of skills and expertise, groups do perform better on the whole (Napier, 1967). The term 'better' needs to be defined, and in this context can be taken to mean to provide a wider range of views and perspectives, to be able to consider a wider range of decision options or solutions, and to give other people (outside of the group) greater confidence that the decision made is the best, given the circumstances.

However, using small groups to solve problems or make decisions comes at a cost. This includes the time of the group members, difficulty in arranging meetings, the high degree of co-ordination needed by group members and the need for an effective leader for the group. We have examined other costs in some detail over the course of this chapter – the dangers of group polarisation and groupthink in particular.

Finally, the fact that we are social animals may mean that the use of groups for problem-solving, decision-making and so on is an inevitable feature of human life – both at a personal level and in organisations such as government, private business and education.

Summary

Decision-making may be characterised as rational or intuitive. Rational involves logic and structured thought; intuitive involves feelings and insights a person may have. Individual decision-makers may be categorised according to the small number of decision-making styles. These are directive, analytic, conceptual and behavioural styles.

Models of decision-making are often classified into one of two types: normative and descriptive. Normative models provide rules and guidelines of how decisions should be approached. Descriptive models attempt to describe what actually happens. An individual decision-maker may use a number of mental short-cuts called 'heuristics of thinking'. These include availability, representativeness, and anchoring and adjustment. Group decision-making has been looked at from the perspective of social decision schemes and group polarisation. Social decision schemes include consensus, unanimity rule, truth wins and majority rule. Group polarisation occurs where the effect of group discussion is to make more extreme the average view of the individuals in the group.

Groupthink is the tendency of a highly cohesive group to make poor-quality decisions because group members spend too much time maintaining the cohesiveness of the group rather than properly evaluating information and the alternatives available. Individuals perform better than groups on simple tasks, but more complex projects require a range of skills and expertise that is rarely found in any one individual.

Further reading

Brown, R. (2000) *Group Processes: Dynamics Within and Between Groups* (2nd edn), Oxford: Blackwell. Updated edition of a well-respected text taking a distinctly European perspective. Provides a wider coverage of groups than this book. Has excellent critical commentaries in places.

Janis, I. (1989) *Crucial Decisions: Leadership in Policy-making and Crisis and Management*, New York: Free Press. Demonstrates the applicability and value of the concept of groupthink to decision-making at a high level in both US government and large business organisations.

Witte, E. and Davis, J. H. (eds) (1996) *Understanding Group Behaviour: Consensual Action by Small Groups*, Hillsdale, NJ: Erlbaum. Good summary of a wide range of aspects of small group behaviour. Extends the treatment of group decision-making given in this chapter.

Glossary

adjourning is the fifth and final stage of group development. It is where a group may disband because it has achieved the task set, or where some members have left the group and need to be replaced before getting on with the task (see also group development).

administrative model of decision-making regards decision-makers as capable of processing only a limited amount of information. This model employs the concepts of bounded rationality and satisficing.

aggregate of people is a collection of unrelated people who happen to be in close proximity for a short period of time (e.g. a football crowd) (see also psychological group).

anchoring and adjustment is a heuristic where a person starts from an initial position or anchor and makes an adjustment in light of subsequent information. Typically an insufficient adjustment is made leaving the anchor point as too influential (see also heuristics of thinking).

availability heuristic is a rule of thumb people use to justify frequency of an event by the ease with which relevant or specific instances can be brought to mind. The examples brought to mind might be biased in some way, leading to an incorrect judgement being made (see heuristics of thinking).

bargaining is where agreement is reached through both groups and individuals in a group giving up something in return for something else (e.g. plea-bargaining in a criminal court) (see also negotiation).

behavioural style is an approach to understanding leadership which focuses on the actual behaviour shown by leaders; for example, Bales showed there often to be two types of leaders in a group: the task-oriented and socio-emotional leaders.

bounded rationality is where the decision-maker simplifies the situation to extract only the essential information regarded as needed to make a decision.

brainstorming is a commonly used technique designed to encourage small groups, both formal and informal, to produce novel and creative ideas and then evaluate the merits of each. A brainstorming group performs less well than the most able individual in the group.

coalition formation is where two or more members of a group form a subgroup and agree to co-operate to achieve mutually desirable outcomes (see also conflict resolution).

coercive power is where the leader is able to threaten or sanction individuals in the group if they do not conform or agree with decisions, judgements or directions that the leader wishes the group to take.

cohesiveness may be seen as the 'glue' that holds a group together. It is the extent to which individuals in the group are attracted to each other and the idea of the group. Very high and very low levels of cohesiveness may be dysfunctional to a group (see also group structure and groupthink).

collective effort model explains social loafing through stating that the individual sees less of a link between effort and outcome, and group performance and individual reward, as group size increases. Because of this, individuals in a group put in less effort (see also social loafing).

collective fences are where high individual costs are avoided by an individual with the consequences of a negative outcome to the group as a whole (e.g. avoiding payment of television licence or car road tax) (see also social dilemmas).

collective traps are situations where a resource is limited and selfish behaviour by an individual is detrimental to the group (see also social dilemmas).

collectivistic is the other extreme to the individualistic dimension for judging cultural difference. Collectivistic cultures value group achievement over individual success (see also individualism).

communication networks are different types of communication structures such as the wheel, chain and circle (see also communication structure).

communication structure refers to how members of a small group are structured to permit communication between themselves (see also communication networks).

conflict resolution may be achieved through specific individual styles of a person, coalition formation and/or escalation of a conflict.

conformity is where individuals fall in line with or conform to the majority view. Conformity is often due to public compliance with the views of others rather than private acceptance (see also majority influence and social influence).

contingency theory of leadership (see leadership effectiveness, least preferred co-worker, situational favourableness).

decision-making styles has been conceptualised by suggesting two different dimensions – ways of thinking and tolerance for ambiguity. These yield four different styles – directive, analytic, conceptual and behavioural styles of decision-making.

deindividuation occurs in larger group settings and is where individual group members lose their personal identity, with the consequence that they feel anonymous and less responsible for their own actions. Deindividuation is associated with loss of individual control, and may lead to riots and mob behaviour.

Delphi technique is where face-to-face interaction between group members is avoided, and ideas and solutions to problems set the group are made anonymously. The ideas/solutions are circulated to each group member for evaluation (see also nominal group technique).

distraction–conflict is an explanation of social facilitation which suggests that performing in front of an audience distracts the individual and causes his or her attention to be divided between the task to perform and the reactions of the audience watching (see also social facilitation).

distributive bargaining is where a fixed amount of resources is divided up, leading to a win–lose outcome for both sides (see also integrative bargaining).

drive theory is an explanation for social facilitation suggested by Zajonc, whereby an audience is assumed to be arousing for the performer, thus increasing the tendency to produce dominant (well-practised) responses (see also social facilitation).

electronic brainstorming is where the brainstorming technique is used and adapted through e-mail and the internet.

environment of small groups refers to the physical, social and temporal contexts in which small groups work and exist.

equality in a small group is where all members of the group are treated equally. Lack of equality of treatment may cause conflict to arise in a group (see also equity in a small group).

equity in a small group refers to rewarding individual members of the group according to the value or achievements or seniority of the members.

escalation of a conflict is where the leader or members of a group bring matters to a head and make the conflict more intense. This is supposed to help resolve conflict since such high levels are not tolerable for long periods (see also conflict resolution).

ethical considerations that need to be taken into account when conducting research on small groups include participant consent, deception, debriefing and confidentiality.

evaluation apprehension is an explanation of why an individual feels aroused when he or she performs in front of an audience. The individual is apprehensive about the evaluation the audience will make of his or her performance (see also social facilitation and drive theory).

expert power is where the leader has superior knowledge and understanding in a specialised area of relevance to the group (see also leadership).

formal groups are usually created by organisations to achieve a task to further the mission of the organisation (see also informal groups).

forming is the initial stage of group development where individuals come together as a group and get acquainted with each other (see also group development).

free-rider effect is where an individual becomes a member of a group, loafs or free-rides through doing little work in the group but enjoys the rewards and achievements of the group (see also social loafing).

'great man' theory of leaders is the idea that leaders are born with or inherit certain characteristics of personality which will make them become a great leader.

group development has been characterised as going through five stages: forming, storming, norming, performing, adjourning. Some groups may go through all five stages, others may not progress beyond a certain stage.

group norms are simply the rules by which a group operates. Group norms may be both prescriptive (guidelines) and proscriptive (what not to do). Norms may be formal or informal (see also group structure).

group polarisation is the tendency of group members, as a result of group discussion, to shift towards a more extreme position that is already held by the group as a whole (see also risky shift).

group size is an important variable that affects performance, communication and cohesiveness of a group. In many situations a group size of between three and eight people is regarded as optimum.

group socialisation occurs when established groups adopt new members who are then socialised into the rules, norms, values and so on of the group. There are five stages associated with group socialisation: investigation, socialisation, maintenance, resocialisation, remembrance.

group structure refers to interrelationships between individuals in a group and includes cohesiveness, norms, status and roles.

groupthink is defective group decision-making resulting from members of the group trying to seek concurrence, consensus and unanimity among themselves rather than looking critically at all options. Tends to be shown by highly cohesive groups operating under time pressures to make a decision.

heuristics of thinking are mental short-cuts that people use or rules of thumb that allow complex information to be highly simplified to arrive at a decision. The three most common heuristics of thinking are availability, representativeness, and anchoring and adjustment.

illusion of group effectiveness is where individuals in the group believe themselves to be more effective than they actually are.

image theory is a model of intuitive decision-making which is based upon an underlying logical approach. This model represents a combination of rational and intuitive decision-making (see also intuitive decision-making and rational decision-making).

individual style of conflict resolution has been seen to result from the concern with the interests of other people and concern with self-interests (see also conflict resolution).

individualism is one important dimension on which cultural differences are perceived to exist, and refers to a culture which values individual achievement and success over collective achievement (see also collectivistic).

informal groups are small groups of people who have a common interest, (e.g. family groups, leisure groups) (see also formal groups).

informational influence is where individuals change their views as a result of new or different information being presented to them (see also normative social influence).

informational power is where the leader has privileged access to certain types of information not available to other members of the group.

initiation rites are rites of passage or tests that a new member of an established group often has to go through to become an accepted member of a group.

integrative bargaining is where both sides seek to maximise potential gains, leading to a win–win situation for both sides (see also distributive bargaining).

Interaction Process Analysis is a systematic approach to the observation, recording and analysis of group behaviour and group communications developed by Robert Bales in the 1950s (see also SYMLOG).

intergroup conflict refers to negative behaviours, actions, prejudice and discrimination that take place between two or more groups.

inter-rater reliability concerns how well different observers, usually two or three, categorise the same behaviour in the same or highly similar ways (see also intra-rater reliability).

intragroup process are behaviours, communications and actions that take place within a small group, between the members of the group.

intra-rater reliability concerns how well the same observer categorises the same behaviour on a numberof different occasions, usually two (see also inter-rater reliability).

intuitive decision-making is where more creative solutions or decisions are required and arrived at through a process that cannot easily be subdivided into logical steps (see rational decision-making).

leader personality refers to the suggestion that all leaders have certain personality traits in common: research generally does not support this, however, talkativeness and high intelligence are two traits common to many leaders.

leadership may be exercised through the use of one or more of five different types of power: reward power, referent power, informational power, legitimate power, expert power, coercive power.

leadership effectiveness was researched by Fiedler who produced a contingency theory of leadership effectiveness. Fielder claimed that leadership effectiveness depended on the behavioural style of the leader and the favourableness of the situation (see also least preferred co-worker and situational favourableness).

least preferred co-worker was used by Fiedler to assess whether a leader was more task-oriented or more socio-emotionally oriented in their leadership style. The former thinks less highly of his or her least preferred co-worker than does the latter (see also leadership effectiveness).

legitimate power refers to the extent to which the members of the group accept that the leader has the right to influence them and take decisions for the group.

majority influence is where the majority view prevails over the minority view or views. Majority influence may be achieved through compliance rather than the majority changing its privately held view (see also normative social and informational influence).

minority influence is where the views of a minority prevail over an opposing or different majority view. Minority influence is usually achieved through informational influence.

negotiation may be defined as communications that take place between opposing groups or members of a group who are in conflict. Offers and counter-offers are made until an agreed solution is reached (see also bargaining).

nominal group technique is a three-stage process where individuals work alone on a problem initially, followed by communication of ideas between group members, and finally, group evaluation. This technique is thought to avoid competition between members of the group and domination by one person in a group (see also brainstorming).

normative social influence is where individuals conform to the majority view. This is usually because the individual or group wants to be liked and accepted by others (see also informational influence).

normative theory of leadership identifies autocratic, consultative and group decision styles of leadership and relates the effectiveness of each style to situational factors of decision quality and group acceptance of leader decisions.

norming is the third stage of group development and is where the group comes together, agrees on things, and a degree of group cohesiveness develops (see also group development).

observer bias is where the researcher knows what the research and research hypothesis is about, and intentionally or unintentionally makes judgements and categorises behaviour in a way likely to support the research hypothesis. Usually avoided by the observer being 'blind' about the purpose of the research.

participant observation is where a person is both a member of a group and an observer, for research purposes, of the group. Typically other members of the group are unaware of the dual role of the participant observer.

path–goal theory of leadership suggests that leaders may adopt one of four leadership styles (directive, supportive, participative, achievement-oriented) according to the situation.

performing is the fourth stage of group development and is where the group gets down to the task or objective it has been set. Groups that have successfully come through the earlier stages of forming, storming and norming usually perform well (see also group development).

prisoner's dilemma is a two-person decision-making game used extensively in psychological research to investigate competition and co-operation between two individuals or two groups.

production blocking is an explanation put forward to explain why brainstorming groups perform worse than the same number of individuals working alone. In effect, the group environment blocks production of ideas because of difficulties in getting opportunities to speak, and forgetting (see also brainstorming).

psychological group is a number of people who interact with each other, are psychologically aware of each other and perceive themselves to be in a group (see also small group).

rational decision-making is where, typically, the decision-making process may be broken down into a number of different steps. One approach is the six-step model.

rational-economic model of decision-making is where the decision-maker is required to identify all possible alternative courses of action available and to rationally assess each to arrive at the correct decision.

referent power is where a leader is looked up to and respected by the other members of the group. Referent power will enable the leader to get members of the group to want to be in and to remain in the group.

reliability of observations concerns how well different observations – either by the same person or other people – of the same behaviour are consistent or in agreement over pre-defined categories (see also inter-rater reliability and intra-rater reliability).

representativeness heuristic is a rule of thumb people use to judge how representative an example or person is of a category or social group. However, this may involve stereotyping, leading to an incorrect or biased judgement being made (see also heuristics of thinking).

reward power applies to leadership and is where the leader is able to influence others in a group by rewarding them in some way. This may be through money or enhancing status. Reward power also implies that leaders can take away a reward as well.

Ringlemann effect refers to social facilitation. Named after the first person, Ringlemann, to investigate and discover the effect of audiences on individual performance.

risky shift is where the group decision, as a result of group discussion, adopts a more risky view or decision than that held by the group members before discussion has taken place (see also group polarisation).

role conflict occurs when an individual occupies different roles in different groups (e.g. family group and work group), and has simultaneous but conflicting demands placed on him or her. Role conflict is highly stressful (see also role strain).

role differentiation is how different people perform different roles in a group and how clearly the different roles can be seen as different or differentiated from each other (see also group structure and role strain).

role strain occurs when an individual experiences difficulty in performing the role that he or she has been given in a group. This may occur because of lack of expertise, low self-confidence or lack of recognition by others (see also role conflict and role differentiation).

roles in a group are the behaviours of individuals occupying different positions in a group. Each role (e.g. leader, expert, communicator) will have norms of behaviour attached to it (see also role differentiation and group structure).

satisficing is where decision-makers are said to select a good enough alternative or course of action, recognising that this may not always represent the best decision that could be made.

self-help groups are normally voluntary groups of people who come together to share needs and common problems (e.g. Alcoholics Anonymous, health groups).

situational favourableness was an assessment by Fiedler of the environment or context in which a leader operated. Situational effectiveness is measured by assessing leader–follower relations, task structure, and position of power of the leader.

small group is regarded as a group of between two and 30 people. Most commonly, small groups vary in size between three to four up to 15 or 20 members (see also psychological group and aggregate).

social decision schemes offer a small number of simple rules shown to be accurate in predicting the final decision of a group based upon knowledge of each group member's initial position. The five rules are unanimity, majority, truth wins, two-thirds majority and first shift.

social dilemmas are situations where each person in a group may act selfishly to maximise his or her own personal gain, or act in the common good of the group. Typically used in situations where there is a scarce or limited resource available to the group.

social facilitation is where individual performance is enhanced for dominant (well-practised) responses and worsened for non-dominant (not well-practised) responses (see also drive theory).

social impact theory explains social loafing by assuming that as group size increases, the social force or impact of each individual is decreased. This means that each individual feels less responsible for the group goal as the group gets larger (see also social loafing).

social influence is actions and communications made by individuals or groups that change the beliefs, attitudes, values or behaviours of others.

social loafing occurs in small groups and is where an individual or individuals in the group work less hard at the task or do not pull their weight. Social loafing has been explained by social impact theory and the collective effort model.

status of an individual in a group refers to his or her standing or position of prestige in a group. Status may be informally and/or formally recognised by the other group members and those external to the group.

storming is the second stage of group development and is where differences between group members over the purpose of the group, the perception of the task set and so on surface. Bargaining may take place in order to arrive at agreement in the group (see also group development).

sucker effect is where an individual in a group thinks that the other group members are not pulling their weight and leaves the individual to do all the work. Often the individual refuses to be 'played for a sucker' (see also social loafing).

SYMLOG is an acronym for a System for the Multiple Level Observation of Groups. SYMLOG can be used across a wide range of different groups. It is based on views of the actual members of a group (see also Interaction Process Analysis).

systematic observation of a group involves careful planning and clear definition of categories of behaviour, attitudes, values, feelings and so on that the researcher wishes to measure. Systematic observations must be reliable (see also reliability).

transformational leaders are leaders who become agents of great social, political and/or economic change. Transformational leaders are charismatic, enthuse others and are visionary.

work group is a formal group set up to achieve a certain task for an organisation. A work group may be enduring or exist only for the project which, when completed, would mean the work group is disbanded (see also formal groups).

References

Agoustinos, M. and Walker, I. (1995) *Social Cognition: An Integrated Introduction*. London: Sage.

Aldag, R. J. and Fuller, S. R. (1993) Beyond fiasco: a reappraisal of the groupthink phenomenon and a new model of group decision processes. *Psychological Bulletin*, 113, 533–552.

Allport, F. H. (1920) The influence of the group upon association and thought. *Journal of Experimental Psychology*, 3, 159–182.

Ancona, D. G. and Caldwell, D. F. (1988) Beyond task and maintenance: defining external functions of groups. *Group and Organizational Studies*, 13, 468–494.

Aronson, E. and Mills, J. (1959) The effects of severity of initiation on liking for a group. *Journal of Abnormal and Social Psychology*, 41, 258–290.

Asch, S. E. (1951) Effects of group pressure upon the modification and distortion of judgements. In: H. Guetzkow (ed.) *Groups, Leadership and Men*. Pittsburgh, PA: Carnegie Press.

Asch, S. E. (1955) Opinions and social pressure. *Scientific American*, 193(5), 31–35.

Asch, S. E. (1956) Studies of independence and conformity: a minority of one against a unanimous majority. *Psychological Monographs*, 70.

Bales, R. F. (1950) *Interaction Process Analysis: A Method for the Study of Small Groups*. Chicago, IL: University of Chicago Press.

Bales, R. F. (1953) The equilibrium problem in small groups. In: T. Parsons, R. F. Bales and E. A. Shils (eds) *Working Papers in the Theory of Action*. New York: Free Press.

Bales, R. F. (1955) How people interact in conferences. *Scientific American*, 192, 31–35.

Bales, R. F. (1970) *Personality and Interpersonal Behaviour*. New York: Holt, Rinehart & Winston.

Bales, R. F. and Cohen, S. P. (1979) *SYMLOG: A System for the Multiple Level Observation of Groups*. New York: Free Press.

Bales, R. F. and Slater, P. (1955) Role differentiation in small decision-making groups. In: T. Parsons (ed.) *Family, Socialization and Interaction Processes*. New York: Free Press.

Baron, R. A. and Byrne, D. (2000). *Social Psychology* (9th edn). Boston: Allyn & Bacon.

Baron, R. S. (1986) Distraction–conflict theory: progress and problems. In: L. Berkowitz (ed.), *Advances in Experimental Social Psychology*, 20. New York: Academic Press.

Baron, R. S., Kerr, N. and Miller, N. (1992) *Group Processes, Group Decision, Group Action*. Milton Keynes: Open University Press.

Baron, R. S., Vandello, V. A. and Brunsman, B. (1996) The forgotten variable in conformity research: impact of task importance on social influence. *Journal of Personality and Social Psychology*, 71, 915–927.

Bass, B. M. (1990) *Bass and Stogdill's Handbook of Leadership* (3rd edn). New York: Free Press.

Bass, B. M. (1997) Does the transactional–transformal leadership paradigm transcend organisational and national boundaries? *American Psychologist*, 52(2), 130–139.

Bass, B. M. and Avioli, B. J. (1993) Transformational leadership: a response to critiques. In: M. M. Chemers and R. Ayman (eds) *Leadership Theory and Research: Perspectives and Directions*. San Diego, CA: Academic Press.

Bavelas, A. (1950) Communication patterns in task-oriented groups. *Journal of Psycholinguistic Research*, 22, 725–730.

Bavelas, A. and Barrett, D. (1951) An experimental approach to organisational communication. *Personnel*, March.

Benne, K. D. and Sheats, P. (1948) Functional roles of group members. *Journal of Social Issues*, 4, 41–49.

Blake, R. R. and Mouton, J. S. (1970) The fifth achievement. *Journal of Applied Behavioural Science*, 6, 413–426.

Blake, R. R. and Mouton, J. S. (1985) *The Managerial Grid III*. Houston, TX: Gulf.

Bond, M. H. and Hwang, K. K. (1986) The social psychology of Chinese people. In: M. H. Bond (ed.) *The Psychology of the Chinese People*. Hong Kong: Oxford University Press.

Bond, R. and Smith, P. B. (1996) Culture and conformity: a meta-analysis of studies using Asch's line judgement task. *Psychological Bulletin*, 119, 111–137.

Bouchard, T. J., Barsaloux, J. and Draudeu, G. (1974) Brainstorming procedure, group size and sex as determinants of the problem-solving effectiveness of groups and individuals. *Journal of Applied Psychology*, 59, 135–138.

Brauer, M., Judd, C. M. and Gliner, M. D. (1995) The effects of repeated expressions on attitude polarisation during group discussion. *Journal of Personality and Social Psychology*, 68, 1014–1029.

Breakwell, G. M., Hammond, S. and Fife-Shaw, C. (eds) (2000) *Research Methods in Psychology* (2nd edn). London: Sage.

Brown, R. (2000) *Group Processes: Dynamics Within and Between Groups* (2nd edn). Oxford: Blackwell.

Buchanan, D. and Huczynski, A. (1997) *Organisational Behaviour: An Introductory Text*. London: Prentice-Hall.

Budescu, D. V., Rappaport, A. and Suleiman, R. (1990) Resource dilemmas with environmental uncertainty and asymmetric players. *European Journal of Social Psychology*, 20, 475–487.

Burnstein, E. (1982) Persuasion as argument in processing. In: H. Brandstatter, J. H. Davies and S. Stocher-Kreichgauer (eds) *Contemporary Problems in Group Decision-Making*. New York: Academic Press.

Butler, D. and Geis, F. L. (1990) Non-verbal affect responses to male and female leaders: implications for leadership evaluations. *Journal of Personality and Social Psychology*, 58, 48–59.

Callaway, M. R., Marriott, R. G. and Esser, J. K. (1985) Effects of dominance on group decision-making: toward a stress-reduction explanation of groupthink. *Journal of Personality and Social Psychology*, 49, 949–952.

Carnevale, P. J. and Pruitt, D. G. (1992) Negotiation and mediation. *Annual Review of Psychology*, 43, 531–582.

Cartwright, D. (1968) The nature of group cohesiveness. In: D. Cartwright and A. Zander (eds) *Group Dynamics: Research and Theory* (3rd edn). New York: Harper & Row.

Cartwright, D. (1971) Risk taking by individuals and groups: an assessment of research employing choice dilemmas. *Journal of Personality and Social Psychology*, 20, 361–378.

Cervone, D. and Peake, P. (1986) Anchoring, efficacy and action: the influence of judgemental heuristics on self-efficacy, judgements and behaviour. *Journal of Personality and Social Psychology*, 50, 492–501.

Chemers, M. M. (1993) An integrative theory of leadership. In: M. M. Chemers and R. Ayman (eds), *Leadership Theory and Research: Perspectives and Directions*. San Diego, CA: Academic Press.

Chemers, M. M., Hays, R. B., Rhodewalt, F. and Wysocki, J. (1985) A person-environment analysis of job stress: a contingency model explanation. *Journal of Personality and Social Psychology*, 49, 628–635.

Cohen. A. R., Fink, S. L., Gadon, H. and Willits, R. D. (1995) *Effective Behaviour in Organisations* (6th edn). Burr Ridge, IL: Irwin.

Conger, J. A. (1991) Inspiring others: the language of leadership. *Academy of Management Executive*, 5, 31–45.

Coolican, H. (1999) *Research Methods and Statistics in Psychology* (3rd edn). London: Hodder & Stoughton.

Cottrell, N. B. (1972) Social facilitation. In: C. G. McClintock (ed.) *Experimental Social Psychology*. New York: Holt.

Cowan, D. A. (1986) Developing a process model of problem recognition. *Academy of Management Review*, 11, 763–776.

Davis, J. H. (1973) Group decision and social interaction: a theory of social decision schemes. *Psychological Review*, 80, 97–125.

Dawes, R. M. (1991) Social dilemmas, economic self-interest, and evolutionary self-interest. In: D. R. Brown and J. E. Smith (eds) *Frontiers of Mathematical Psychology: Essays in Honour of Clyde Coombs*. New York: Springer-Verlag.

De Castro, J. M. and Brewer, E. M. (1991) The amount eaten in meals by humans is a power function of the number of people present. *Physiology and Behaviour*, 51, 121–125.

De Dreu, C. K. W. and McCusker, C. (1997) Gain–loss frames and co-operation in two-person social dilemmas: a transformational analysis. *Journal of Personality and Social Psychology*, 72, 1093–1106.

De Dreu, C. K. W. and Van Lange, P. A. M. (1995) Impact of social value orientation on negotiation cognition and behaviour. *Personality and Social Psychology Bulletin*, 21, 1178–1188.

De Gilder, D. and Wilke, H. A. M. (1994) Expectation states theory and motivational determinants of social influence. *European Review of Social Psychology*, 5, 243–269.

Delbecq, A. L., Van De Veu, A. H. and Gustafson, D. H. (1975) *Group Techniques for Program Planning*. Glenview, IL: Scott, Foresman.

Denmark, F. L. (1980) Psyche: from rocking the cradle to rocking the boat. *American Psychologist*, 35, 1057–1065.

Dennis, A. R. and Valacich, J. S. (1993) Computer brainstorms: more heads are better than one. *Journal of Applied Psychology*, 78, 531–537.

Deutsch, M. and Coleman, P. T. (2000) *Handbook of Conflict Resolution: Theory and Practice*. San Francisco, CA: Jossey-Bass.

Diehl, M. and Stroebe, W. (1987) Productivity loss in brainstorming groups: towards the solution of a riddle. *Journal of Personality and Social Psychology*, 53, 497–509.

Diehl, M. and Stroebe, W. (1991) Productivity loss in idea-generating groups: tracking down the blocking effect. *Journal of Personality and Social Psychology*, 61, 392–403.

Dion, K. L., Baron, R. and Miller, N. (1970) Why do groups make riskier decisions than individuals? In: L. Berkowitz (ed.) *Advances in Experimental Social Psychology, Volume 5*. New York: Academic Press.

Dubrovsky, V. J., Keisler, S. and Sethna, B. N. (1991) The equalization phenomena: status effects in computer-mediated and face-to-face decision-making groups. *Human Computer Interactions*, 6, 119–146.

Eagly, A. H. and Johnson, B. T. (1990) Gender and leadership style: a meta-analysis. *Psychological Bulletin*, 108, 233–256.

Eagly, A. H., Karau, S. J. and Makhijani, M. G. (1991) Gender and the emergence of leaders: a meta-analysis. *Journal of Personality and Social Psychology*, 60, 685–710.

Eagly, A. H., Makhijani, M. G. and Klonsky, B. G. (1992) Gender and the evaluation of leaders: a meta-analysis. *Psychological Bulletin*, 111, 3–22.

REFERENCES

Eisenstat, R. A. (1990) Compressor team start up. In: J. R. Hackman (ed.) *Groups That Work (And Those That Don't)*. San Francisco, CA: Jossey-Bass.

Esser, J. K. (1998) Alive and well after 25 years: A review of groupthink research. *Organizational Behaviour and Human Decision Process*, 73, 116–141.

Feldman, D. C. (1984) The development and enforcement of group norms. *Academy of Management Review*, 9, 47–53.

Festinger, L. (1957) *A Theory of Cognitive Dissonance*. Stanford, CA: Stanford University Press.

Fiedler, F. E. (1965) A contingency model of leadership effectiveness. In: L. Berkowitz (ed.) *Advances in Experimental Social Psychology*, *Volume 1*. New York: Academic Press.

Fiedler, F. E. (1971) *Leadership*. Morristown, NJ: General Learning Press.

Fiedler, F. E. (1978) Contingency model and the leadership process. In: L. Berkowitz (ed.) *Advances in Experimental Social Psychology*, *Volume 11*. New York: Academic Press.

Fiedler, F. E. (1981) Leadership effectiveness. *American Behavioural Scientist*, 24, 619–632.

Fodor, E. M. (1976) Group stress, authoritarian style of control and use of power. *Journal of Applied Psychology*, 61, 313–318.

Fraser, C., Gouge, C. and Billig, M. (1971) Risky shifts, cautious shifts and group polarisation. *European Journal of Social Psychology*, 1, 7–30.

Frederickson, J. W. and Mitchell, T. R. (1984) Strategic decision processes: comprehensiveness and performance in an industry with an unstable environment. *Academy of Management Journal*, 27, 399–423.

French, J. R. P. and Raven. B. H. (1959) The bases of social power. In: D. Cartwright (ed.) *Studies in Social Power*, Ann Arbor, MI: Institute for Social Research.

Frost, D. F. and Stahelski, A. J. (1988) The systematic measurement of French & Raven's bases of social power in workgroups. *Journal of Applied Social Psychology*, 18, 375–389.

Gallupe, R. B., Bastianatti, L. M. and Cooper, W. H. (1991) Unblocking brainstorms. *Journal of Applied Psychology*, 76, 137–142.

Gebhardt, L. J. and Meyers, R. A. (1995) Subgroup influence in decision-making groups: examining consistency from a communication perspective. *Small Group Research*, 26, 147–168.

Geen, R. G. and Gange, J. J. (1983) Social facilitation: drive theory and beyond. In: H. H. Blumberg, A. P. Hare, V. Kent and M. Davies (eds) *Small Groups and Social Interaction, Volume 1*. London: Wiley.

Greenberg, J. and Baron. R. A. (1993) *Behaviour in Organisations* (5th edn). Boston, MA: Allyn & Bacon.

Greenberg, J., Williams, K. D. and O'Brien, M. K. (1980) Considering the harshest verdict first: biasing effects of mock-juror verdict. *Personality and Social Psychology Bulletin*, 12, 41–50.

Griffit, W. B. (1970) Environmental effects on interpersonal affective behaviour: ambient effective temperature and attraction. *Journal of Personality and Social Psychology*, 15, 240–244.

Gross, N., Mason, S. W. and McEarchen, A. W. (1958) *Explorations in Role Analysis*. New York: Wiley.

Guetzkow, N. and Simon, H. A. (1955) The impact of certain communication networks on organisation and performance in task-oriented groups. *Management Science*, 1, 233–250.

Hall, J. (1971) Decisions, decisions, decisions. *Psychology Today*, November, 86–88.

Harrison, E. F. (1995) *The Managerial Decision-Making Process* (4th edn). Boston, MA: Houghton-Mifflin.

Heilman, M. E., Hornstein, H. A., Cage, J. H. and Herschlag, J. K. (1984) Reactions to prescribed leader behaviour as a function of role perspective: the case of the Vroom-Yelton model. *Journal of Applied Psychology*, 69, 50–60.

Hemphill, J. K. (1950) Relations between the size of a group and the behaviour of 'superior' leaders. *Journal of Social Psychology*, 32, 11–22.

Hofstede, G. (1980) *Culture's Consequences: International Differences in Work-related Values*. Beverly Hills, CA: Sage.

Hofstede, G. (1983) Dimensions of national cultures in fifty countries and three regions. In: J. Deregowski, S. Dzvirawiec and R. Annis (eds) *Expications in Cross-Cultural Psychology*. Lisse, NL: Swetz & Zeitlinger.

Hogg, M. A. (1992) *The Social Psychology of Group Cohesiveness: From Attraction to Social Identity*. London: Harvester Wheatsheaf.

House, R. J. and Baetz, M. L. (1979) Leadership: some generalisations and research directions. In: B. M. Staur (ed.) *Research in Organizational Behaviour*. Greenwich, CT: J.A.I. Press.

House, R. J., Spangler, W. D. and Woycke, J. (1991) Personality and charisma in the U.S. presidency: a psychological theory of leadership effectiveness. *Administrative Science Quarterly*, 36, 364–396.

Howell, J. M. and Frost, P. J. (1989) A laboratory study of charismatic leadership. *Organisational Behaviour and Human Decision Processes*, 43, 243–269.

Janis, I. (1982) *Groupthink: Psychological Studies of Policy Decisions and Fiascos*. Boston, MA: Houghton-Mifflin.

Janis, I. (1989) *Crucial Decisions: Leadership and Policy-Making in Crisis and Management*. New York: Free Press.

Janis, I. and Mann, L. (1977) *Decision-Making: A Psychological Analysis of Conflict, Choice and Commitment*. New York: Free Press.

Jewell, L. N. and Reitz, H. J. (1981) *Group Effectiveness in Organisations*. Glenview, IL: Scott, Foresman.

Johnson, R. D. and Downing, L. L. (1979) Deindividuation and valence of cues: effects on pro-social and anti-social behaviour. *Journal of Personality and Social Psychology*, 37, 1532–1538.

Jorgenson, D. O. and Papciak, A. S. (1981) The effects of communication, resource feedback, and identifiability on behaviour in a simulated commons. *Journal of Experimental Social Psychology*, 17, 373–385.

Kabanoff, B. (1991) Equity, equality, power and conflict. *Academy of Management Review*, 16, 416–441.

Kanas, N. (1985) Psychological factors affecting simulated and actual space missions. *Aviation, Space and Environmental Medicine*, 56, 806–811.

Karau, S. J. and Williams, K. D. (1993) Social loafing: a meta-analytic review and theoretical integration. *Journal of Personality and Social Psychology*, 65, 681–706.

Kelley, H. H. and Stahelski, A. J. (1970) Social interaction basis of co-operators and competitors' beliefs about others. *Journal of Personality and Social Psychology*, 16, 66–91.

Kephart, W. M. (1950) A quantitative analysis of intergroup relations. *American Journal of Sociology*, 60, 544–549.

Kerr, N. L. and Braun, S. (1981) Ringlemann revisited: alternative explanations for the social loafing effect. *Personality and Social Psychology Bulletin*, 7, 224–231.

Kerr, N. L. (1983) Motivation losses in small groups: a social dilemma analysis. *Journal of Personality and Social Psychology*, 45, 819–828.

Kerr, N. L., Garst, J., Lewandowski, D. A. and Harris, S. E. (1997) That still, small, voice: commitment to co-operate as an internalised versus a social norm. *Personality and Social Psychology Bulletin*, 23, 1300–1311.

Key, N. (1986) Abating risk and accidents through communication. *Professional Safety*, 31(11), 25–28.

Kiesler, S. and Sproull, L. (1992) Group decision-making and communication technology. *Organisational Behaviour and Human Decision-Making Processes*, 52, 96–123.

Killian, L. M. (1952) The significance of multiple-group membership in disaster. *American Journal of Sociology*, 57, 309–313.

Kinder, D. R. and Sears, D. O. (1985) Public opinion and political action. In: G. Lindzey and E. Aronson (eds) *Handbook of Social Psychology* (3rd edn). New York: Random House.

Kirkpatrick, S. A. and Locke, E. A. (1991) Leadership: do traits matter? *Academy of Management Executive*, 5(2), 48–60.

Kogan, N. and Wallach, M. A. (1964) *Risk Taking: A Study in Cognition and Personality*. New York: Holt.

Krantz, J. (1985) Group processes under conditions of organisational decline. *Journal of Applied Behavioral Science*, 21, 1–17.

Kravitz, D. A. and Martin, B. (1986) Ringlemann rediscovered: the original article. *Journal of Personality and Social Psychology*, 32, 1134–1146.

Latané, B. and Nida, S. (1980) Social impact theory and group influence: a social engineering perspective. In: P. B. Paulus (ed.) *Psychology of Group Influence*. Hillsdale, NJ: Erlbaum.

Latané, B., Williams, K. and Harkins, S. (1979) Many hands make light work: the causes and consequences of social loafing. *Journal of Personality and Social Psychology*, 37, 822–832.

Laughlin, P. R. and Ellis, A. L. (1986) Demonstrability and social combination processes on mathematical intellective tasks. *Journal of Experimental Social Psychology*, 22, 177–189.

Leavitt, H. J. (1951) Some effects of certain communication patterns on group performance. *Journal of Abnormal and Social Psychology*, 46, 38–50.

Lee, C. (1991) Followership: the essence of leadership. *Training*, 28, 27–35.

Levine, J. M. and Moreland, L. (1995) Group processes. In: A. Tesser (ed.) *Advanced Social Psychology*, New York: McGraw-Hill.

Levine, J. M. and Moreland, R. L. (1998) Small groups. In: D. T. Gilbert, S. T. Fiske and G. Lindzey (eds) *The Handbook of Social Psychology* (4th edn). New York: McGraw-Hill.

Levy, L. H. (1979) Processes and activities in groups. In: M. A. Liebermann and L. D. Borman (eds) *Self-Help Groups for Coping with Stress*. San Francisco, CA: Jossey-Bass.

Lewin, K. (1947) Frontiers in group dynamics. *Human Relations*, 1, 5–42.

Lewis, S. A., Langan, C. J. and Hollander, E. P. (1972) Expectation of future interaction and the choice of less desirable alternatives in conformity. *Sociometry*, 35, 440–447.

Lippett, R. and White, R. (1943) The 'social climate' of children's groups. In: R. G. Barker, J. Kounin and H. Wright (eds) *Child Behaviour and Development*. New York: McGraw-Hill.

Luce, R. D. and Raiffa, H. (1957) *Games and Decisions*. New York: Wiley.

McClelland, D. C. (1965) Toward a theory of motive acquisition. *American Psychologist*, 20, 321–333.

Mann, R. D. (1959) A review of the relationship between personality and performance in small groups. *Psychological Bulletin*, 56, 241–270.

March, J. G. and Simon, H. A. (1958) *Organisations*. New York: Wiley.

Messick, D. M. and Brewer, M. B. (1983) Solving social dilemmas. In: L. Wheeler and P. Shaver (eds) *Review of Personality and Social Psychology, Volume 4*. Beverly Hills, CA: Sage.

Messick, D. M., Wilke, H., Brewer, M. B., Kramer, R. M., Zemke, P. E. and Lui, L. (1983) Individual adaptations and structural change as solutions to social dilemmas. *Journal of Personality and Social Psychology*, 44, 294–309.

Miles, J. A. and Greenberg, J. (1995) Using punishment threats to alternate social loafing effects among swimmers. *Organisational Behaviour and Human Decision Processes*.

Miller, C. E. (1989) The social psychological effects of group decision rules. In: P. B. Paulus (ed.) *Psychology of Group Influence* (2nd edn). Hillsdale, NJ: Erlbaum.

Miller, C. E. and Komorita, S. S. (1986) Coalition formation in organisations: what laboratory studies do and do not tell us. In: R. J. Lewicki, B. H. Sheppard and M. H. Buzerman (eds) *Research on Negotiation in Organisations, Volume 1*. Greenwich, CT: JAI Press.

Misumi, J. (1985) *The Behavioural Science of Leadership: An Interdisciplinary Japanese Research Programme*. Ann Arbor, MI: University of Michigan Press.

Mitchell, T. R. and Beach, L. R. (1990) 'Do I love thee? Let me count . . .' Toward an understanding of intuitive and automatic decision-making. *Organisational Behaviour and Human Decision Processes*, 47, 1–20.

Mitchell, T. R., Rothman, M. and Liden, R. C. (1985) Effects of normative information on task performance. *Journal of Applied Psychology*, 70, 48–55.

Moreland, R. L. and Levine, J. M. (1982) Socialisation in small groups: temporal changes in individual-group relations. In: L. Berkowitz (ed.) *Advances in Experimental Social Psychology, Volume 15*. New York: Academic Press.

Moreland, R. L. and Levine, J. M. (1984) Role transitions in small groups. In: V. Allen and E. Van de Vliert (eds) *Role Transitions: Explorations and Expectation*. New York: Plenum Press.

Moreland, R. L. and Levine, J. M. (1988) Group dynamics over time: development and socialisation in small groups. In: J. E. McGrath (ed.) *The Social Psychology of Time: New Perspectives*. Newbury Park, CA: Sage.

Moreland, R. L. and Levine, J. M. (1989) Newcomers and old timers in small groups. In: P. B. Paulus (ed.) *Psychology of Group Influence*. Hillsdale, NJ: Erlbaum.

Moscovici, S. (1985) Social influence and conformity. In: G. Lindzey and E. Aronson (eds) *Handbook of Social Psychology* (3rd edn). New York: Random House.

Muczyk, J. P. and Reimann, B. C. (1987) The case for directive leadership. *Academy of Management Review*, 12, 647–687.

Mugny, G., Kaiser, C. *et al.* (1984) Intergroup relations, identification and social influence. *British Journal of Social Psychology*, 23, 317–322.

Mugny, G. and Pérez, J. A. (1991) *The Social Psychology of Minority Influence*. Cambridge: Cambridge University Press.

Mullen, B. J. (1986) Atrocity as a function of lynch mob composition: a self-attention perspective. *Personality and Social Psychology Bulletin*, 12, 187–197.

Mullen, B. J., Chapman, J. and Satas, E. (1989) Effects of group composition: 'Lost in the crowd' or 'centre of attention'. *Revista Latino Americana de Psycologia*, 21, 43–55.

Mullen, B. J., Johnson, C. and Satas, E. (1991) Productivity loss in brainstorming groups: a meta-analytic integration. *Basic and Applied Social Psychology*, 12, 3–27.

Mullen, B., Salas, E. and Driskell, J. E. (1989) Salience motivation and artefact as contributions to the relation between participation rate and leadership. *Journal of Experimental Social Psychology*, 25, 545–549.

Napier, H. (1967) Individual versus group learning: note on task variables. *Psychological Reports*, 23, 757–758.

Napier, R. W. and Gershenfeld, M. K. (1999) *Groups: Theory and Experience* (6th edn). Boston, MA: Houghton Mifflin.

Neale, M. and Bazerman, M. (1991) *Cognition and Rationality in Bargaining*. New York: Free Press.

Nemeth, C. J. (1995) Dissent as driving cognition, attitudes and judgements. *Social Cognition*, 13, 273–291.

Osborn, A. F. (1957) *Applied Imagination*. New York: Scribners.

Palich, L. and Hom, P. W. (1992) The impact of leader power and behaviour on leadership perceptions. *Group and Organizational Management*, 17(3), 279–296.

Pascale, R. T. and Athos, A. G. (1982) *The Art of Japanese Management*. Harmondsworth: Penguin Books.

Paulus, P. B. (1998) Developing consensus about groupthink after all these years. *Organizational Behaviour and Human Decision Processes*, 73, 362–374.

Paulus, P. B. and Dzindolet, M. T. (1993) Social influence processes in group brainstorming. *Journal of Personality and Social Psychology*, 64, 575–586.

Paulus, P. B., Dzindolet, M. T., Poletes, G. and Camacho, L. M. (1993) Perception of performance in group brainstorming: the illusion of group productivity. *Personality and Social Psychology Bulletin*, 19, 78–89.

Pennington, D. C. (2000) Social dilemmas: individual choice versus group needs. *Psychology Review*, 6, 2–5.

Pennington, D. C., Gillen, K. and Hill, P. (1999) *Social Psychology*. London: Arnold.

Pennington, N. and Hastie, R. (1990) Practical implications of psychological research on juror and jury decision-making. *Personality and Social Psychology Bulletin*, 16, 90–105.

Pessin, J. (1933) The comparative effects of social and mechanical stimulation on memorizing. *American Journal of Psychology*, 45, 263–270.

Peters, L. H., Harke, D. D. and Pohlmau, J. T. (1985) Fielder's contingency theory of leadership: an application of the meta-analytic procedures of Schmidt and Hunter. *Psychological Bulletin*, 97, 274–385.

Peterson, M. F. *et al.* (1995) Role conflict, ambiguity and overload: a 21 nation study. *Academy of Management Journal*, 38, 429–452.

Principle, C. D. and Neeley, S. E. (1983) Nominal versus interactive groups: further evidence. *Atlantic Journal of Business*, 22, 25–34.

Pruitt, D. G. and Carnevale, P. J. (1993) *Negotiation in Social Conflict*. Pacific Grove, CA: Brooks/Cole.

Pruitt, D. G. and Rubin, J. Z. (1986) *Social Conflict: Escalation, Stalemate, and Settlement.* New York: Random House.

Pruitt, D. G., Carnevale, J. D., Ben-Yoav, O., Nochajski, T. H. and Van Slyck, M. R. (1983) Incentives for co-operation in integrative bargaining. In: R. Tietz (eds) *Aspiration Levels in Bargaining and Economic Decision-Making.* Berlin: Springer-Verlag.

Rahim, M. A. (1983) A measure of styles of handling interpersonal conflict. *Academy of Management Journal,* 26, 368–376.

Raven, B. H. (1993) The bases of social power: origins and recent developments. *Journal of Social Issues,* 49, 227–251.

Reicher, S. D. (1987) Crown behaviour as social action. In: J. C. Turner, M. A. Hogg, P. J. Oakes, S. D. Reicher and M. S. Wetherell *Rediscovering the Social Group: A Self-Categorisation Theory.* Oxford: Blackwell.

Reitzes, D. C. and Diver, J. K. (1982) Gay bars as deviant community organisations: the management of interaction with outsiders. *Deviant Behaviour,* 4, 1–18.

Rice, R. W. (1978) Construct validity of the least preferred co-worker score. *Psychological Bulletin,* 85, 1199–1237.

Rogelberg, S. G., Barnes-Farrell, J. L. and Love, C. A. (1992) The stepladder technique: an alternative group structure facilitating effective group decision-making. *Journal of Applied Psychology,* 77(5), 730–737.

Ross, L. (1977) The intuitive psychologist and his shortcomings. In: L. Berkowitz (ed.) *Advances in Experimental Social Psychology, Volume 10.* New York: Academic Press.

Ross, L. and Ward, A. (1995) Psychological barriers to dispute resolution. In: M. P. Zanna (ed.) *Advances in Experimental Social Psychology, Volume 27,* San Diego, CA: Academic Press.

Rothman, A. J. and Hardin, C. D. (1997) Differential use of the availability heuristic in social judgement. *Personality and Social Psychology Bulletin,* 23, 123–138.

Rowe, A. J., Bougarides, H. and McGrath, M. R. (1984) *Managerial Decision-Making.* Englewood Cliffs, NJ: Prentice-Hall.

Sanders, G. S. (1983) An attentional process model of social facilitation. In: H. H. Blumberg, A. P. Hare, V. Kent and M. Davies (eds) *Small Groups and Social Interaction, Volume 1.* London: Wiley.

Schmitt, B., Gilovich, T. K., Goore, N. and Joseph, L. (1986) Mere presence and social facilitation: one more time. *Journal of Experimental Social Psychology,* 22, 242–248.

Schriesham, C. A. and De Nisi, A. S. (1981) Task dimensions as moderators of the effects of instrumental leadership: a two sample replicated test of path–goal leadership theory. *Journal of Applied Psychology*, 66, 589–597.

Schweiger, P. M., Sandberg, W. R. and Ragan, J. W. (1986) Group approaches for improving strategic decision-making: a comparative analysis of dialectical enquiry, devil's advocate and consensus. *Academy of Management Journal*, 29, 51–71.

Secord, P. F. and Backman, C. W. (1974) *Social Psychology* (2nd edn). Tokyo: McGraw-Hill.

Senge, P. M. (1990) *The Fifth Discipline: The Art and Practice of the Learning Organization*. New York: Doubleday.

Seta, C. A. and Seta, J. J. (1992) Increments and decrements I: mean arterial pressure levels as a function of audience composition: an averaging and summation analysis. *Personality and Social Psychology Bulletin*, 18, 173–181.

Shaw, M. E. (1981) *Group Dynamics: The Social Psychology of Small Group Behaviour* (3rd edn). New York: McGraw-Hill.

Sherif, M., Harvey, O. J., White, B. J., Hood, N. and Sherif, C. (1961) *Intergroup Conflict and Co-operation: The Robber's Cave Experiment*. Norman, OK: University of Oklahoma Institute of Intergroup Relations.

Simon, H. A. (1957) *Models of Man*. New York: Wiley.

Simon, H. A. (1976) *Administrative Behaviour* (3rd edn). New York: Free Press.

Simon, H. A. (1979) Rational decision-making in organisations. *American Economic Review*, 69, 493–513.

Simonton, D. K. (1994) *Greatness: Who Makes History and Why?* New York: Guilford Press.

Slater, P. E. (1955) Role differentiation in small groups. *American Sociological Review*, 20, 300–310.

Smith, P. B. and Bond, M. H. (1998) *Social Psychology Across Cultures* (2nd edn). London: Prentice Hall.

Stahelski, A. J., Frost, D. E. and Patch, M. E. (1989) Use of socially dependent bases of power: French and Raven's theory applied to workgroup leadership. *Journal of Applied Social Psychology*, 19, 283–297.

Stang, D. J. (1972) Conformity, ability and self-esteem. *Representative Research in Social Psychology*, 3, 97–103.

Stogdill, R. (1974) *Handbook of Leadership*. New York: Free Press.

Stoner, J. A. F. (1961) *A Comparison of Individual and Group Decisions Including Risk*. Masters thesis, Massachusetts Institute of Technology.

Strasser, G. M. (1992) Pooling of unshared information during group discussion, In: S. Worchel, W. Wood and J. H. Simpson (eds) *Group Processes and Productivity*. Newbury Park, CA: Sage.

Strasser, G. M., Taylor, L. A. and Hanna, C. (1989) Information sampled in structured and unstructured discussion of three- and six-person groups. *Journal of Personality and Social Psychology*, 57, 67–78.

Stroebe, W. and Diehl, M. (1994) Why groups are less effective than their members: on productivity losses in idea-generating groups. In: W. Stroebe and M. Hewstone (eds) *European Review of Social Psychology, Volume 5*, New York: Wiley.

Stroebe, W., Diehl, M. and Abakoumkin, G. (1992) The illusion of group effectivity. *Personality and Social Psychology Bulletin*, 18, 645–650.

Strube, M. J. and Garcia, J. E. (1981) A meta-analytic investigation of Fiedler's contingency model of leadership effectiveness. *Psychological Bulletin*, 90, 307–321.

Sundstrom, E. (1986) *Workplaces: The Psychology of the Physical Environment in Offices and Factories*. Cambridge: Cambridge University Press.

Taylor, D. W., Berry, P. C. and Block, C. H. (1958) Does group participation when using brainstorming facilitate or inhibit creative thinking? *Administrative Science Quarterly*, 3, 23–47.

Tesser, A. (1995) *Adanced Social Psychology*. New York: McGraw Hill.

Tetlock, P. E., Peterson, R. S., McGuire, C., Chang, S. and Feld, P. (1992) Assessing group dynamics: a test of the groupthink model. *Journal of Personality and Social Psychology*, 63, 403–425.

The British Psychological Society (1998) *Code of Conduct, Ethical Principals and Guidelines*. Leicester: The British Psychological Society.

Thibaut, J. W. and Kelley, H. H. (1959) *The Social Psychology of Groups*. New York: Wiley.

Thomas, K. W. (1976) Conflict and conflict management. In: M. D. Dunnette (ed.) *Handbook of Industrial and Organisational Psychology*. Chicago, IL: Rand McNally.

Thompson, L. (1993) The impact of negotiation on intergroup relations. *Journal of Experimental Social Psychology*, 29, 304–325.

Thompson, L. (1995) They saw a negotiation: partnership and involvement. *Journal of Personality and Social Psychology*, 68, 839–853.

Thompson, L. (1998) *The Mind and Heart of the Negotiator*. Upper Saddle River, NJ: Prentice-Hall.

Ting-Toomey, S., Gao, G. and Trubisky, P. (1991) Culture, face maintenance and styles of handling interpersonal conflict. *International Journal of Conflict Management*, 2, 275–296.

Tjosvold, D. (1984) Effects of leader warmth and directiveness on subordinate performance on a subsequent task. *Journal of Applied Psychology*, 69, 222–232.

Triplett, N. (1898) The dynamogenic factors in pacemaking and competition. *Journal of Psychology*, 9, 507–533.

Tuckman, B. (1965) Development sequences in small groups. *Psychological Bulletin*, 63, 384–399.

Turner, J. C. and Oakes, P. J. (1989) Self-categorisation and social influence. In: P. B. Paulus (ed.) *The Psychology of Group Influence* (2nd edn). Hillsdale, NJ: Erlbaum.

Turner, J. C., Wetherell, M. S. and Hogg, M. A. (1989) Referent information influence and group polarisation. *British Journal of Social Psychology*, 28, 135–147.

Turner, M. E., Pratkanis, A. R., Probasco, P. and Leve, C. (1992) Threat, cohesion and group effectiveness: testing a social identity maintenance perspective on groupthink. *Journal of Personality and Social Psychology*, 63, 781–796.

Tversky, A. and Kahneman, D. (1973) Availability: a heuristic for judging frequency and probability. *Cognitive Psychology*, 5, 207–232.

Tversky, A. and Kahneman, D. (1982) Judgement under uncertainty: heuristics and biases. In: D. Kahneman, P. Slovic and A. Tversky (eds) *Judgement Under Uncertainty*. New York: Cambridge University Press.

Van Der Vliert, E., Euwema, M. C. and Huismans, S. E. (1995) Managing conflict with a subordinate or a superior: effectiveness of conglomerated behaviour. *Journal of Applied Psychology*, 80, 271–281.

Van Dijt, E. and Wilke, H. (1993) Differential interests, equity and public good provision. *Journal of Experimental Social Psychology*, 29, 1–16.

Vancouver, J. B. and Ilgen, D. R. (1989) Effects of interpersonal orientation and the sex-type of the task on choosing to work alone or in groups. *Journal of Applied Psychology*, 74, 927–934.

Vaught, C. and Smith, D. L. (1980) Incorporation and mechanical solidarity in an underground coal mine. *Sociology of Work and Occupations*, 7, 159–187.

Vroom, V. H. and Jago, A. G. (1978) On the validity of the Vroom-Yelton model. *Journal of Applied Psychology*, 63, 151–162.

Vroom, V. H. and Yelton, P. W. (1973) *Leadership and Decision-Making.* Pittsburgh, PA: University of Pittsburgh Press.

Walton, R. E. and McKersie, R. B. (1965) *A Behavioural Theory of Labour Negotiations: An Analysis of a Social Interaction System.* New York: McGraw-Hill.

Weeks, D. (1992) *The Eight Essential Steps to Conflict Resolution.* New York: Putnam.

Welton, G. L. and Pruitt, D. G. (1987) The mediation process: the effects of mediator bias and disputant power. *Personality and Social Psychology Bulletin,* 14, 123–133.

Wilkinson, J. (2000) Direct observation. In: G. M. Breakwell, S. Hammond and C. Fife-Shaw *Research Methods in Psychology* (2nd edn). London: Sage.

Williams, K. D. and Karau, S. J. (1991) Social loafing and social compensation: the effects of expectations of co-worker performance. *Journal of Personality and Social Psychology,* 61, 570–581.

Williams, K. J., Suls, J., Alliger, G. M., Learner, S. M. and Wan, C. K. (1991) Multiple role juggling and daily mood states in working mothers: an experience sampling method. *Journal of Applied Psychology,* 76, 633–638.

Witte, E. and Davis, J. H. (eds) (1996) *Understanding Group Behaviour: Consensual Action by Small Groups.* Hillsdale, NJ: Erlbaum.

Wofford, J. C. and Liska, L. Z. (1993) Path–goal theories of leadership: a meta-analysis. *Journal of Management,* 857–876.

Wuthnow, R. (1994) *Sharing the Journey: Support Groups and America's New Quest for Community.* New York: Free Press.

Yamaguchi, S., Okamato, K. and Oka, T. (1985) Effects of co-actor's presence: social loafing and social facilitation. *Japanese Psychological Research,* 27, 215–222.

Yukl, G. (1994) *Leadership in Organisations* (3rd edn). Englewood Cliffs, NJ: Prentice-Hall.

Zaccaro, S. J., Foti, R. J. and Kenny, D. A. (1991) Self-monitoring and trait-based variance in leadership: an investigation of leader flexibility across multiple group situations. *Journal of Applied Psychology,* 76, 308–315.

Zajonc, R. B. (1965) Social facilitation. *Science,* 149, 269–274.

Zallow, H. M. and Seligman, M. E. P. (1990) Pessimistic rumination predicts defeat of presidential candidates 1900 to 1984. *Psychological Enquiry,* 1, 80–85.

Zimbardo, P. G. (1970) The human choice: individuation, reason and order versus deindividuation, impulse and chaos. In: W. J. Arnold and D. Levine (eds) *Nebraska Symposium on Motivation, Volume 17.* Lincoln: University of Nebraska Press.

Zuber, J. A., Croft, H. W. and Werner, J. (1992) Choice shift and group polarisation: an analysis of the status of arguments and social decision schemes. *Journal of Personality and Social Psychology,* 65, 50–61.

Index